JUST BENEATH THE SURFACE

The Processes of Counseling and Psychotherapy

Dr Sandra Delroy

in collaboration with

Cheryl Gordon

Copyright © Sandra Delroy 1996

First published in 1996 in London, England
by Dobro Publishing
3 Northumberland House
237 Ballards Lane
London N3 1LB

Typeset in New Baskerville by
Marriott Design and Productions
5 Glebe Crescent, London NW4 1BT

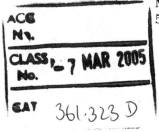
Printed in England by
THE BOOK FACTORY
35/37 Queensland Road
London N7 7AH
(0171) 700 1000

TABLE OF CONTENTS

Introduction

The spirit of this book has to do with an unsophisticated and straightforward description of the ways I work with people who consult with me about the emotional aspects of their lives, and along with that a description of what I teach to health and mental health professionals. It may be that many other counselors and therapists work in similar ways, in which case I speak for many of us coincidentally. To be honest and frank, though, I can only speak for myself. Having worked as a clinical psychologist over a number of years, it is time for me to take stock of what I do.

I invite people to get to know themselves in a particular kind of way. I introduce people to their inner world of emotions. For me, this is a privilege and a truly rewarding experience. Clients gradually get a sense of the way they have neglected their emotional lives and estranged themselves from their core feelings. That part, not only has to do with pain, sadness and anger, but also joy, pleasure, delight and at times a feeling that for now I feel okay. The journey has all sorts of possibilities. It is within the arena of emotional life that a sort of creativity is released. It is this creativity that is capable of enriching one's total existence.

I have been fortunate over the last few years to practise as a clinical psychologist with the Enfield Community Care NHS Trust in England. Within the psychology department I have been provided with support and back-up to allow me to work psychotherapeutically with people who have physical disabilities. I have also been training health professionals, particularly community district nurses, physiotherapists, occupational therapists, as well as junior doctors, mental health nurses, health visitors, psychologists and chiropodists.

For those readers who may have consulted with me, let me assure you at the outset that I will not be presenting any material in these pages that could identify a particular person. In this book, I will do precisely what we did not do in our work together - I will generalise to give others the flavor of what work on one's emotional life is like. Those who have seen me at work know that a general view in no way substitutes for the unique nature of the work, but I want to write a book, and at the same time protect what is confidential. I will compromise by speaking in the general. I will not compromise the confidentiality I established with anyone.

My Personal Clinical Training

When I first started to explore the idea of developing a career in mental health I was living in Cleveland, Ohio, having found myself there during some years of travel and uncertainty. I started reading the counseling and psychotherapy literature, initially discovering Carl Rogers' (1951) work, and I volunteered in a short-stay psychiatric unit. I returned home to London for one year and volunteered as a counselor with The Samaritans, a large organization that operated primarily for suicide prevention.

At this time, in 1971, I had not decided where to live, the UK or the USA. I applied for social work training in England, was accepted, and then was told I could not begin after all, since a tutor had suddenly resigned so ten students were put off and I was among them. One tutor resigned and that changed my life.

I was disappointed and fed up so I returned to Cleveland, Ohio, which by now felt like home, and began again. By that time I had a work visa, and soon after was granted immigrant status, and I worked with a medico-legal consultant, focusing on medical malpractice. Early in 1973, I commenced studies at a two-year college, Cuyahoga Community College, with a view to becoming a mental health technician. During the first quarter I realized that instead of a two-year degree, I preferred to study psychology and work towards a doctorate in clinical psychology. I received my doctorate (Psy.D) early in 1984 from The Illinois School of Professional Psychology, with an undergraduate degree in psychology and M.A. in educational psychology, along the way, both from John Carroll University in Cleveland.

The turning point for me probably had to do with the educational atmosphere I discovered Downtown Cleveland at Cuyahoga Community College. I was a mature student, as were many of us. The encouragement and feedback from faculty members, who were dedicated educators, enabled me to work very hard and achieve good results. They provided me with the necessary stimulation to persevere towards the goals I had set for myself, and they taught me how to study. That was a memorable time of my life, because this was the first educational institution I had been associated with that was facilitative for me.

Everything that I studied was relevant and I committed myself to the learning process as I moved on to John Carroll University and later The Illinois School of Professional Psychology.

Along the way, in between undergraduate and graduate work, I was employed for a couple of years as a counselor for a large comprehensive mental health center Downtown Cleveland. I worked primarily with the long-term chronic mentally ill. The standards set by the center, Community Guidance and Human Services were high, and it was there that I learned basic clinical skills, working with clients. The emphasis was very much on reaching out to clients who were suspicious and afraid of mental health agencies.

Working closely with a psychiatrist in the center, enabled me to develop facilitative skills in counseling relationships with people who for so long had been labeled as having schizophrenia and other psychotic disorders. We were able to provide emotional support for people who were struggling to survive. There were frustrations in journeying along with clients and facing with them the many obstacles, often bureaucratic, that stopped them from progressing; and of course there were the obstacles that came from within as well, long-standing conflicts and difficulties that they had been unable to resolve, due perhaps, at least partially, to insufficient counseling input over the years. Treatment in the past had mostly been limited to psychotropic medication. I was lucky to work with a psychiatrist who valued supportive psychotherapy and prescribed carefully.

At the end of 1979 I moved to Chicago where I had been offered a place at The Illinois School of Professional Psychology to complete the Psy.D.degree. It was there that I learned how to be a professional psychologist. It was the influence of Marc Lubin, Mary Hendricks, Judith Flaxman and Jim McHolland that most deeply affects the way I work. The coursework was intense as were the seminars and supervision. I was able to explore theoretical and clinical aspects of working psychotherapeutically. Philosophically, The Illinois School suited me well. The emphasis, just as it had been at Cuyahoga Community College, and Community Guidance Human Services, was on providing services for clients that were facilitative, and that respected their dignity.

During the first year of training, students had to demonstrate competency in person-centered therapy. I had worked as a counselor for some time before moving to Chicago and was amazed to see that I had not yet learned to listen properly. Despite my voluntary and work experience, it really was like starting again. Being nondirective turned out to be far more difficult than I had realized. I was fortunate to be in a School where the level of acceptable competency was high enough that I never felt that I was simply going through the motions, and I acquired the theoretical and practical expertise to practise psychotherapy. There was so much to learn, I had to hold on so as not to lose confidence, and I survived.

I was on placement at a junior school and did supervised psychotherapy with children in my second year. The model I used was client-centered. The main area of competency to be attained in the second year was the psychotherapy assessment, the initial interview. I will always be grateful for having been able to devote an entire academic year to beginning psychotherapy relationships. It was also beneficial to focus on more than one approach, so that in addition to having acquired client-centered skills, I felt competent working behaviorally, and psychodynamically with individuals, couples and families. Coursework remained heavy with pressure of exams always in view, and the pressure of having to pass comprehensive examinations was now imminent.

The third year focused on acquiring competency in ongoing psychotherapy, and my orientation had to be declared so that I could be examined from that perspective. It had been very hard for me to settle on my psychotherapeutic orientation. I had been through phases of veering towards a behavioral approach, steering away from the person-centered approach because I did not take on board all aspects of it. I began psychoanalytic courses with a good deal of scepticism, believing psychoanalysis to be responsible for attitudes in society which did not sit well with me. My impression of psychoanalysis was that it contributed to sexism, racism, authoritarianism, and I was suspicious of it because it had a secret language which I did not readily understand. Why do so many psychoanalysts speak in code? Not only that, there seemed to be a certain dogmatism among them that had the flavor of a religious cult. Perhaps it's the nod nod-wink wink feel of it that made me reject it for so long. Also, I had never met anyone who had seemed to benefit from it.

In order to decide my psychotherapeutic orientation I attended seminars for a year coming from each of the major orientations. In psychoanalytic psychotherapy courses I struggled with aspects that made no sense to me, determined to be able to work that way before rejecting it. Marc Lubin was the faculty member who taught courses on psychoanalysis and he spoke plain language. Not only that, he made sure students understood it well enough to write papers, and clinical analyses, in understandable and accurate language. He eradicated for me the main obstacle. I didn't have to speak a new language. I also learned that it was not psychoanalysis *per se* that was racist and sexist. One did not have to be prejudiced and discriminating in order to become a psychoanalyst. I had somehow stereotyped them in that way. It seemed like I was making some headway. I could work as a psychoanalytic psychotherapist without changing my values and attitudes towards people.

The final decision was based on studying the work of Margaret Mahler (1968). It was evident that there was a vast body of psychoanalytic literature describing important work that had been carried out with people at different stages of life, focusing on developmental issues in ways that other approaches did not. The literature on learning theory emphasized intellectual and moral development, but it was psychoanalysis that enabled us to study and observe emotional development.

I had become a declared psychoanalytic psychotherapist. I followed the communicative approach that was developed by Robert Langs (1974) and was supervised according to that model. The approach was entirely consistent with my philosophy of facilitating clients' processes. It allowed me, in perhaps a somewhat unorthodox way, to combine what I saw as the best of person-centered therapy with the most relevant aspects of psychoanalytic thinking that seemed pertinent to people wanting to actively work on their emotional development, whether or not there had been an onset of symptoms.

An "American" Clinical Psychologist Practising in London, England

Having completed my training I eagerly returned home to London where I had planned to practise as a clinical psychologist. I remember as a psychology undergraduate student in a developmental psychology course, the lecturer described how one progresses from reaching the top, only then to start something new and find oneself, once more, at the bottom.

Subsequently, I came crashing down in London with the help of society and the British clinical psychology profession. I knew that my training had been excellent. However, it transpired that being a clinical psychologist in America was totally different from being a clinical psychologist in Britain. It was as if they were two separate professions.

I started the conversion from an American clinical psychologist to a British one in 1982 but gave up quite early on, deciding it would be better for me to remain an American one, since they worked primarily as psychotherapists. Although British clinical psychologists have since moved in that direction, they are a much smaller profession, relatively speaking, and there was a marked difference between the professional self-esteem of the two professional groups. I opted to stay in the group with high self-esteem. That choice left me somewhat isolated.

It was unfortunate for me on a personal level that my reception by the British profession was not warmer. My earlier educational experiences in Britain had not been positive, and I had hoped that my clinical expertise would have been more readily welcomed. The situation worsened when I discovered that British clinical psychologists were for the most part excluded from treating inpatients in psychiatric units. I persevered on a particular unit, although the psychiatrists mostly ignored me, and undermined my input. It was a miserable time for me.

I was working psychotherapeutically with a number of inpatients, and some, who had not communicated with staff before, except in aggressive or withdrawn ways, entered into working relationships with me. However, their progress was not attributed to my input by the psychiatric staff, since they had decided years ago to disregard any significant therapeutic input from clinical psychologists for what is known as 'political' reasons. That is the polite way of saying that they were so set in their ways, it was too risky to let in non-medical staff for fear that they would be more effective in patient care. Unfortunately, British clinical psychologists took much longer than my American counterparts to play an important part in mental health settings, and were often squeezed out by their psychiatrist colleagues.

Having survived the early eighties in London, I have since established myself as a senior member of the profession and gradually I became accepted, along with my American ways. Sometimes I feel that I am more American than Americans in terms of how deeply I internalized many American values. What I appreciated most was the ability many Americans had with regard to communicating clearly and directly, including how they felt about whatever they were saying. I learned how to improve my interpersonal skills socially with Americans. For example, they handled introductions and introducing themselves so well. People were rarely left standing nameless among a group of people. I found them to be well-mannered and hospitable.

The characteristics outlined above may seem superficial. They are over-generalizations, but it was these behaviors that impressed me. There were enough people around for me with those characteristics that enabled me to learn from them, internalize the skills, and value the importance of how they could be used in daily interactions thereby increasing mutual understanding. My idealization of America is due to my gratitude to them for educating me in a way that was not available for me in Britain. In some ways, I feel I was born in the wrong country. That is not to say that while living in America I had no complaints. The American educational system certainly suited me very well. I returned to England to be with my family, and to come back home.

When I started working in the health service part of my job was to supervise people of various disciplines in the psychological aspects of their work. It soon became apparent that while most mental health professionals were very confident about the theoretical underpinnings of whatever discipline they were in, they found themselves faltering as counselors because their training programs had only included a few lectures on that aspect of their work. In fact, they had been told while training not to worry about their skills since they would pick them up as they went along. What many people I saw were concerned about was that they had picked up some bad habits. It was quite early on that I recognized a need for counseling skills training, and I started offering workshops and courses nationally in 1986. They were very well received and continue to meet a need among health and mental health professionals, social workers, medical practitioners, voluntary agency workers, and educators.

This book is directed primarily to health and mental health professionals, graduate and postgraduate students in clinical, counseling, and educational psychology, social work, physical therapy, physiotherapy, recreational therapy, occupational therapy, nursing, medicine, and the various professional groups allied to medicine. It is also likely to be of interest to an educated audience already well-exposed to popular psychology and psychotherapy literature. It is hoped that it will help many people, whether or not they are working in health, education, or social work, to better understand the complexities of emotional life. A glossary has been prepared to broadly define what the jargon means to this writer.

Chapters Two, Three and Four provide the background and bias of the book. The second chapter ("Why Bother With Personal Growth Through

Self-Exploration?") equates the importance of attending to one's mind and body, thereby giving the rationale for personal growth work, and leading into the third chapter ("Person-Centered Therapy-The Background") which provides the context in which person-centered therapy developed. As an 'American' clinical psychologist practising in London, England, the fourth chapter ("Who Are The Potential Facilitators of Personal Growth in the UK?") describes the discrepancy in levels of expertise of the various groups available to the general public, for their mental health care.

Chapters Five, Six, Seven, Eight and Nine focus in detail on numerous aspects of psychotherapeutic work. The fifth chapter ("Assessment, Facilitation, Or Both?") focuses on the initial session(s) bringing together a nondirective person-centered approach and a psychodynamic way of coming to understand the client's psychotherapeutic needs so that appropriate recommendations can be made. The sixth chapter ("Emotions, And The Way We Feel About Them") is a comprehensive chapter covering Rogerian notions of 'experiencing beings', and the 'uniqueness of the individual', and outlines some psychological concepts to do with needs, conflicts, tension reduction and frustration tolerance from the psychoanalytic, behavioral and humanistic perspectives, before elaborating on anxiety and depression.

The seventh chapter ("Communicating Verbally and Nonverbally With Clients") highlights the importance of the counselor's verbal skills, the value of silence, and the difficulties for clients in gaining some level of accuracy in communicating feelings, which are nonverbal. The eighth chapter ("On Bereavement") exemplifies how the principles discussed in the book can be used in work with those who have been bereaved. The ninth chapter ("Why is the Psychotherapeutic Relationship *Different* From All Other Relationships?") gives a comprehensive account of its importance in various therapeutic orientations, but I particularly demonstrate how I have reconciled the person-centered and psychoanalytic approaches in the way I use the relationship in therapy.

The tenth and eleventh chapters describe the way I teach the five-day course and its content. I discuss the sorts of issues health and mental health professionals bring, and the way I teach them how to improve their listening skills, as well as help them undergo an attitudinal shift in terms of understanding the importance of emotional life. Also, in this chapter considerable space is devoted to a detailed description of the complexities involved in acknowledging clients' *emotional life* in an empathic way, being sensitive to their private worlds and to their strengths and defences so as to allow them to be in touch with themselves, at least just beneath the surface. A personal account of a past participant on the five day course stands alone in the final chapter, followed by her poem, both written by Cheryl Gordon, a freelance writer, who has collaborated with me in the preparation of the manuscript.

The book is best read in the order of the chapters, inasmuch as each chapter assumes the previous ones have been read. It is my hope that the strength of this book is the way difficult concepts are explained using commonplace examples *via* the vignettes and within the body of the text. Complex psychotherapeutic issues have been described in plain language. An attempt has been made to avoid jargon, and to describe psychological concepts with the same clarity that I aim to convey in my psychotherapeutic work with clients, and to those I teach.

I have spoken about the encouragement I received from American educators and mental health professionals, and I am pleased now to be able to acknowledge the way my British colleagues, in mental health settings as well as general health, finally came through for me so that I have been able to get enormous satisfaction from the way I work in England as a clinical psychologist.

Why bother with Personal Growth through Self-exploration?

Most people want symptom relief and they want it now. It is not surprising since symptoms can be wholly unpleasant. What I have to offer, and others in my line of work, is not an immediate magical solution, but an offer, usually, to engage with the individual in a process of self-exploration to facilitate his or her personal growth. But I do not use these words for they are meaningless to people in distress. 'Personal growth' and 'self-exploration' represent the jargon of a particular school of psychotherapy but are not limited to humanistic psychotherapy. Self-exploration is also an appropriate way of thinking about at least part of the psychoanalytic process.

In my own work, I have brought together a person-centered way of working psychotherapeutically with people in distress, arising out of Carl Rogers' (1961) humanistic approach, and psychoanalytic technique more closely linked to the communicative approach which began with the work of Robert Langs (1974).

Rogers (1961) is important to me because of his detailed study of the elements that make up the characteristics of a helping relationship. He spent half a century examining and re-examining this process. His attention to *empathy, congruence and unconditional positive regard* has enabled me and many other therapists to offer individuals a kind of working relationship which is inherently honest, open, and has as its goal the client's increased understanding of self. Other therapists who are not influenced by him would say they provide the same sort of relationship to their clients, but this has not been validated and certainly I do not believe it.

Langs (1978) is important to me because he works at an unconscious level with the client, and has shown how the client unconsciously communicates to the therapist conflicts, feelings, fantasies, and wishes that are presently being experienced in relation to the therapist as a result of transference or non-transference. He has shown the importance of decoding the client's unconscious derivatives and interpreting only when the client has provided a bridge. Both Rogers and Langs demonstrate a depth of sensitivity towards their clients and genuinely respect the client's process rather than imposing their own selves inappropriately.

Neither of them allows their clients' sessions to be invalidated by the therapist's 'need to be clever'. These therapists recognize that the client is in some deeply personal process which requires facilitation. The best way to be with the client, then, is nondirective, and it is the nondirective element of Rogers' (1961) and Langs' (1978) therapeutic approaches that I use in my work, and I believe it is being nondirective that is most helpful to clients.

Personal growth has to do with an increased understanding of self with a view to change. *Change* is something which is usually resisted and that is what makes psychotherapy so very complex and challenging. *Self-exploration* is the process of becoming familiar with inner conflicts, wishes, anxieties, fears, hopes, dreams, and the way the individual *interacts* in relationships. *Interaction* has to do with one's feelings about self as well as others, and it takes place simultaneously on at least two levels. On the one hand, the individual is interacting internally within his or her own self. Conflicts, wishes, anxieties, fears, and hopes impact continuously within one's self. On the other hand, and at the same time, the individual interacts with other people, so that in addition to the impact of the continuous internal emotional state, one then has feelings, attitudes, and characteristic behaviors that are experienced in relation to others. I prefer to speak about interaction as *the way we are in relationships*, taking into account both individual and interpersonal factors, as described above.

So why bother with personal growth through self-exploration? This question needs to be addressed before anyone can wholeheartedly embark on such a process. Personal growth or change can enable people to make more informed choices and decisions in life, allowing them to be more in control of their destiny. It is for people wanting to take an active part in their day-to-day lives, rather than waiting passively for whatever may befall them.

Personal growth results in people feeling more integrated. It is not unusual for people who have *not* been through this process to feel 'all over the place' inside and unable to describe the way they feel. Awareness of such discomfort may only arise when a person is under considerable stress. At other times, it may not be an issue as to whether or not there exists an inner feeling of wholeness or integration.

Personal growth work can help people become more accepting of all aspects of themselves. There is a tendency to disown bits of ourselves that we do not like. Personal growth allows for the reunion of individual characteristics, feelings, and attitudes after having more deeply understood each of them in their own right. They can then be reintegrated into the total personality in a more constructive and acceptable fashion.

For example, in personal growth work in therapy, people often discover that they are highly critical of others. The way they may have reacted to that vague feeling in the past was to focus on how much other people criticized them. What has happened here is that the fact of feeling critical towards others has been turned inside out, rather than integrated, so that such people complain bitterly about other's criticisms of them.

Being criticized is a regular feature of living. Some people who, perhaps, are not too critical of others, do not get as upset by excessive criticism as do those who are highly critical. The problem with examples is that they can easily be taken as generalizations. Let me make it clear that I am not saying that those who get upset when criticized have to be highly critical people themselves. What I am saying is that the difference between a strong or a mild reaction to someone else's behavior sometimes has to do with whether or not it unconsciously reminds one of an aspect of self that the individual cannot tolerate.

Personal growth work has the advantage of letting an individual know more about those parts of self that are troublesome, so that less time is wasted complaining about that trait in others. Instead, the person can take hold of the unwanted trait, for example, of being excessively critical of others, and better understand its origins, as well as what is maintaining the associated attitudes, feelings and behaviors.

In order to change some part of oneself, it is necessary first to become familiar with it. Familiarization can reduce the fear of it, and even create the opportunity of feeling some compassion towards it. Feeling critical of others usually includes critical feelings towards oneself. Changing one's attitudes towards self and others can be constructive. Instead of berating self and others harshly, alternative ways of evaluating self and others may be found which are less destructive.

Destructive components can be eradicated once they have been identified and understood. This is not a quick, simple procedure, but it is an example of why some people bother with personal growth. It allows for the possibility of living a less conflicted and more easily understandable life.

As a result of personal growth work, it is possible to learn more about how an individual protects himself or herself against pain, and what usually triggers off pain in the first place. We do not all respond in the same way to experiences and events. What is painful for one person may not be for another, and the ways individuals defend against it vary tremendously. Each of us is unique. We develop our own individual ways of protecting ourselves against experiences and events that cause us varying degrees of emotional pain and discomfort.

It makes good sense for people to take care of themselves. In our society it is perfectly acceptable to take reasonable measures to look after oneself, to exercise in the gym, to jog, to attend to one's diet and nutrition and generally to be mindful of having respect for one's body. If only there was a similar attitude towards looking after our emotions. The response to a person attending weekly psychotherapy sessions is not usually the same as to the person who attends weekly exercise sessions. In fact, people in psychotherapy prefer not to tell others they are looking after their emotional lives. Experience has shown them that society frowns upon this activity, believing it to arise from some failure or shortcoming of the individual.

Let us be sure we understand what is going on here. Society would have us believe that it is okay for our bodies to need quite a bit of effort in maintaining efficiency, but our emotional development, apparently, should take care of itself. But that is not the whole story. Not only should our emotions be self-sufficient, society would have us remain ignorant of the contents of emotional life. Emotions, it seems, are problematic extras that must be coped with in life, while we are permitted the freedom to fully experience and understand our bodies. What a double standard!

Of course, it makes good sense to equally look after one's emotional life and one's body. This is undoubtedly a difficult task within an unsympathetic environment. To add to the difficulties, society is not entirely separate from us, because each of us contributes to the make-up of it. Therefore, individuals in psychotherapy very often share society's negative view of the psychotherapeutic process and thus arrive with an added burden or symptom. I am referring here to the madness of a society which assumes that anyone in psychotherapy is there because of failure, inability to cope, or serious emotional problems that cannot be normal. That means that the psychotherapy process is inevitably slowed down by the work that has to be done on the person's self-concept which has been severely damaged by society's insane attitudes towards emotional health.

It seems to me that in the early school years more attention could be paid to emotional development. Included in the curriculum could be some group work where children are encouraged to reflect on their feelings and to engage in self-exploration. It would not be so difficult then in adulthood to experience important life events in a more complete way. Presently, adults are faced with needing to learn difficult interpersonal skills relatively late in life, when their defences against certain sets of feelings have already solidified. School counselors ideally should be available to help children work through their conflicts and improve *the way they are in relationships*.

Everyone can benefit from personal growth work. All that is needed is simply a wish to self-explore and work on one's emotional development. It is neither necessary nor desirable to wait for the onset of symptoms or difficulties. Personal growth work is for people who respect the fact of being human and who recognize the responsibilities that entails both to themselves and to the people they love. Self-exploration can result in the discovery of better ways of living and reaching one's true potential with due regard and consideration for the rights of others. It can provide an increased awareness of who you are and what you are experiencing.

Person-Centered Therapy: The Background

Person-centered therapy has to do with emotional health. It is not about disease, but about living up to one's potential and experiencing self and the world in which one lives fully. The person-centered approach has to do with valuing self and others. Best of all it is about being true to one's self. I will begin by providing some background information about its origins and development, and describe its relation to other major counseling approaches.

In psychology there are three main schools of psychotherapy: *psychoanalytic, behavioral, and humanistic (person-centered).*

Psychoanalysis began at the end of the nineteenth century with the work of Sigmund Freud (1963). He focused on unconscious processes. Practitioners using that approach call themselves psychoanalysts, psychoanalytic psychotherapists, and psychodynamic psychotherapists. Interventions tend to be interpretive focusing on the transference. In the early 1900's, psychoanalysis was practised in the UK initially only by medically-trained doctors, but before Freud's death, at his direction, also by non-medical qualified psychoanalysts.

Behavior therapy began with the work of John Watson (1930) in 1920 and was developed over the last sixty years by B.F.Skinner (1971), based on principles of classical and operant conditioning. Behavior change was effected by manipulating an independent variable and implementing various reward contingencies in order to shape desired behaviors. By the 1940's, behaviorism was quite popular in the United States and probably got started ten or fifteen years later in the UK.

Since the 1960's, *cognitive behavior therapy* became the most popular form of behavior therapy as practised by Aaron Beck (1976), Arnold Lazarus (1981), and Albert Ellis (1973). Cognitive behavior therapy incorporated stimulus-response theories, and introduced cognition as a mediating variable. Rationale-emotive therapy and assertiveness training are cognitive behavioral approaches.

Humanistic psychology was often referred to as the Third Force in psychology. Abraham Maslow (1970) was the father of the humanistic school and was best known for his theory of self-actualization.

Carl Rogers (1957) who was a contemporary of Maslow, developed *client-centered therapy*, which he later called *person-centered therapy*, within the humanistic school. He was trying to get away from the words "patient" and "client". Rogers' (1951) client-centered therapy began in the late 1940's. His work revolved around three core conditions: *congruence*, *empathy*, and *unconditional positive regard*.

First there was and, of course, remains the *medical model* out of which psychiatry came. The medical model is one which gathers together information so as to make a diagnosis. It seeks to group symptoms together in order to classify various illnesses. From the medical and psychiatric models came such labels as 'schizophrenic', 'hysterical', and 'personality disorder', where the doctor or psychiatrist tended to assume a paternalistic and omnipotent stance in relation to the patient. The doctor was the one to tell the patient what to do - to prescribe. Until the 1960's the psychoanalyst also tended to assume a paternalistic and omnipotent stance in relation to the patient. The patient would wait submissively for the analyst's 'wise' interpretation. In a similar vein, behavior therapists see themselves as educators. They believe their job to be one of teaching their clients how to cope better with their lives. They teach new behaviors to their clients.

In humanistic psychology, the relationship with the client was quite different. While the other approaches were, in those days, known to be directive, client-centered therapy was *nondirective*. The therapists took the lead from the client. They listened attentively to their clients in an endeavor to understand the client as a whole person. The relationship was client-centered because the client was seen to be playing the most important role in the dyad, working through his or her process and the therapist was there primarily *to facilitate* that process. No longer, then, was the therapist behaving as an omnipotent figure. If the client felt that way about the therapist, it was the client's creation. The therapist was no longer taking on a paternalistic role, but was instead permitting clients to express themselves *assertively, frankly, and honestly.*

Many practitioners would have been reluctant to adopt that kind of role in relation to their patients. Client-centered therapy would not have been very popular with them. It wasn't and it still isn't in the UK. Client-centered therapy was, however, particularly popular in the United States. It continues to be one of the major psychotherapeutic approaches.

Rogers (1957) developed it in university settings so that it became one of the most popular types of therapy practised in the United States. The most important contribution that I believe it made was its availability to the masses. In the UK it is still developing and is not widely available. For example, only a very few, if any, clinical psychologists, would declare a person-centered orientation. British clinical psychologists tend to be cognitive behavior therapists, psychoanalytic psychotherapists and family therapists.

I've already indicated that practitioners back in the '40's and '50's would have been unlikely to welcome a person-centered therapeutic approach which de-emphasised their status as 'the doctor' or 'the therapist'. Let me describe how Carl Rogers (1961) managed to gain the respect and credibility that he has, and how he managed to have a major influence over the kinds of therapies already being practised.

Carl Rogers was born in 1902 in the USA. He studied clinical psychology at Columbia University, obtaining his M.A. degree and Ph.D. by the time he was twenty-nine years old. He worked for twelve years in the Child Study Department of the Society for the Prevention of Cruelty to Children, in Rochester, New York. He wrote his first book, the *Clinical Treatment of the Problem Child* and in 1940 was offered his first university appointment, a full professorship at Ohio State University. In 1942, his book *Counseling and Psychotherapy: New Concepts in Practice* was published followed by many more books, now considered classics in the field of counseling, throughout his life. He died in 1987 at the age of eighty-five still actively engaged in person-centered therapy using it throughout the world in an attempt to resolve conflict and improve communication.

Rogers followed a respectable and traditional route in making himself academically acceptable. He was a professor of psychology in prestigious American universities. The psychology departments were large and resourceful and conducive to enlarging on the therapeutic model he had already developed. He was able to engage in considerable research to help validate his therapeutic model and thus became recognised, respected and most influential.

I believe Carl Rogers was responsible for a major shift in the attitudes and techniques of therapists of differing orientations. Many psychoanalysts today come across as far less omnipotent in the relationships they develop with their patients. Many have become better listeners and more empathic. They have learned how to be more sensitive to the feelings their patients are working with, and psychoanalytic theory does not teach these very important aspects of the therapy process, but Rogers did.

In fact, when newly qualified doctors or other non-psychologists apply for the psychoanalytic training, they are encouraged to acquaint themselves with the work of Carl Rogers before undertaking psychoanalytic studies or practice. Also, since the mid-sixties, in the US, many behaviorists have acknowledged the importance of empathy and sensitive listening before embarking on a treatment program with their patients (Goldfried and Davison, 1976). In the UK, person-centered therapy has not made much impact. It is difficult to find a professionally trained person-centered counselor excepting in a few places where there are person-centered training centers, particularly Norwich, Norfolk.

I think the relatively small number of person-centered therapists has to do with the fact that there is more elitism in the UK, and it has been harder for the smaller number of practitioners (relative to Americans) to give up their old paternalistic habits and embrace a more human, holistic relationship with clients. The British culture does not encourage this kind of interaction and many psychologists and psychotherapists have rejected it. However, new professions are growing very rapidly - counseling psychology and counseling. Those would be the most likely groups to make more headway with person-centered counseling, but that has not been so. Most of what I have seen tends to be any one of the approaches mentioned earlier, but very little truly person-centered work.

Having described some of the background to person-centered therapy, it is interesting to consider why it seems to have been more difficult to develop this way of working in the UK. It seems to me that the climate in the UK - politically, socially and economically, has not lent itself to a personal growth culture. In the sixties, America was particularly receptive to a psychology that emphasized freedom to choose, identity, self-knowledge and self-appreciation. These were horrible times for many young Americans having to go fight a war in Vietnam that they did not support.

The peace movement was strong and so was the voice of many Americans who said "No," in a variety of ways to injustices within their society.

Ironically, it was some young men from Liverpool in England, known as The Beatles who many Americans responded to as somehow recognizing, and artistically expressing their plight, as well as their hopes. By contrast, in the UK, the peace movements and fights for causes reflect a harsher nature of society. The tendency to reflect on one's feelings in a kinder way appears to be more difficult to come across.

In my own personal experience in England, I gravitate towards groups standing for democratic rights, justice for all, and equality. However, I have felt very uncomfortable in those settings because most group members are highly intellectualized and politicized, with very little interest in staying with deep feelings. What is important in that environment seems to be limited to winning arguments and debates. On the other hand, in America, I found that people were much more able to switch from intellectual conversation to a more reflective style that came from their feelings, rather than confining themselves to their thoughts.

I continue to be hopeful that nondirective approaches to counseling will eventually be more widely taught and understood throughout the health and mental health professions, social services, education, and voluntary organizations. Allowing clients to find their own way in counseling, taking a nondirective stance, in my view results in recovering deeper levels of self-esteem, more self-confidence, and more trust in their own experience. In the end, clients develop more self-respect with the recognition that these changes have come from themselves.

Who are the Potential Facilitators of Personal Growth in the UK?

Who indeed? In Britain there is a health service consisting of numerous professional groups, but very little time is spent, if any, on counseling skills and developmental psychology, when training doctors and other health professionals. When a member of the public takes on the role of patient or client, a member of any one of these disciplines may be seen depending on to whom the initial referral was made. Often, the first contact is with a physiotherapist or a speech therapist, in which case either therapist becomes the *potential facilitator of personal growth*. Everyone is likely, at some time or another, to need the services of a health professional. The health professional will probably be using, either knowingly or unknowingly, counseling skills as a part of the work with the patient. In other words, health professionals can potentially provide the setting necessary for self-exploration and personal growth.

However, there are difficulties. The therapist may know very little about personal growth, so that the possibility of facilitation with patients or clients seen is highly improbable. It is a matter of luck as to whether or not the first health professional seen can respond "professionally" to the emotional aspects presented to them as part and parcel of the patient's overall concerns. For example, a patient recently diagnosed as having a degenerative disease such as multiple sclerosis will most likely have come expecting to be able to describe his or her feelings to the therapist concerning the condition and to be understood within the context of the patient's total personality.

In this chapter, I will first describe what happens to an individual's emotional process when the attending health professional has very little or no psychological background or training. The remainder of the chapter will focus on the complications around which member of which professional group is likely to be seen when a patient is referred solely for assessment and psychotherapeutic intervention relating to emotional issues. To whom does the patient get referred? The possibilities include, but are not limited to, a clinical psychologist, a counseling psychologist, a counselor, or a community psychiatric nurse.

Counseling is a secondary part of health professionals' duties

There is a whole body of health professionals who may be using counseling as a secondary part of its work including rheumatologists, anesthetists, people practising the Alexander technique, chiropracters, osteopaths, acupuncturists, homeopaths; physiotherapists working with people in pain and/or with physical disabilities, speech therapists, district nurses, occupational therapists, health visitors, community nurses, staff nurses and auxiliaries, and charge nurses and sisters working on respite care units, as well as social workers, care assistants and voluntary agency workers.

Each of these professional groups works with people with a variety of problems, including strokes, head injuries, multiple sclerosis and numerous other physical conditions. Any of these community health professionals can do home visits. If there are other medical complaints, neurologists, rheumatologists, or other specialists can be seen in hospital outpatient clinics. People can go to disability centers for physiotherapy or they may receive outpatient physiotherapy in a general hospital.

People who are concerned about their health expect and deserve professional expertise. When people come to clinics or hospitals for care, they quite rightly expect that their feelings as well as their physical conditions will receive attention. They usually assume that health professionals are knowledgeable about most areas of health, including emotional health.

What normally happens is that anxieties, concerns and fears are off-loaded, with the belief that health professionals are equipped to deal with them, or at the very least that they have more understanding of emotional life from a professional perspective than their patients. While people deserve a holistic approach, it also seems reasonable to be faced with a practitioner who has more background in psychology and counseling than the average person in the street. When they find that health professionals are unable to deal with the emotional aspects of their physical complaints, that often leads to disappointment and confusion, leaving their feelings stifled and repressed. In this way, emotional complications can take root. While the feelings probably were quite accessible, people are *taught* to push them back. That is how unwanted psychological symptoms often develop.

Push back feelings

The person resorts to focusing only on his or her body, since, very often, the underlying message from health professionals is that the associated feelings will have to take care of themselves. The frustration experienced by health professionals in these situations has to do with feelings of inadequacy. Many of them do recognize the psychological training gap in their own professional development. Some overcompensate by smothering distressed patients with reassurance. Others try to distance themselves because they do not know what else to do.

The problem of knowing to which discipline to refer

If, as is sometimes necessary, a person needs to be seen by a qualified counselor or psychotherapist, the responsibility for the referral will fall upon the health professional. For example, if a physiotherapist hears how conflicted and troubled the patient is about relationships at home and other issues, it will be important for the physiotherapist to have enough information about counseling and psychotherapy and the options open to the patient, to say that these sound like the sort of issues that are best dealt with by a qualified counselor. It would then be appropriate for the physiotherapist to offer to liaise with the patient's family doctor or general practitioner (GP) (as he or she is known in the UK) for a referral. If it is too much to ask for all health professionals to be taught about the nature of emotional life, at least time should be taken to familiarize them with appropriate referral routes.

Unfortunately, an additional problem exists. Referral routing may not be straightforward so both the patient and referrer will require considerable patience and perseverance. The perseverance will probably pay off and is preferable to leaving the patient without access to counseling or psychotherapy.

I want to turn now to the complexities involved when an individual is referred for counseling or psychotherapy. There are two major areas to explore: (1) will the client be referred to a member of a particular discipline, e.g., clinical psychology, counseling psychology, counseling, community psychiatric nursing, social work, psychiatry, psychotherapy? and (2) what does the client have the right to expect in terms of the competency of the counselor?

Qualified or unqualified, that is the question

The key person to make a counseling referral is the general practitioner. GPs are expected to act as the central agent in all of their patients' health care. In the United States, members of the public are free to see whichever doctor they choose, without needing their family doctors to assess whether or not a referral is indicated.

Therefore, the first obstacle people in the UK face when they decide they want help with their emotional health is having to try to explain it to a doctor. I have already described the lack of psychological training GPs and other health professionals receive. Yet again, the person is exposed to pot luck when the GP is asked to refer them for counseling or psychotherapy. Some GPs talk their patients out of it, either by minimizing their patients' concerns, or offering betablockers in the case of anxiety, or antidepressants if they are feeling sad.

Many patients come away believing that the GP was right. Counseling would not be useful, and it is better not to delve, not to know oneself. GPs often warn their patients that self-exploration could stir their feelings up, resulting in severe emotional problems. It seems to me that they transmit their own fears and ignorance about emotional life and processes to their patients, who are then denied the opportunity of working on their emotional growth. How many GPs would even consider banning their patients from the gym if they needed physical exercise?

To whom should the referral be made?

The GP may, however, be enthusiastic about the prospect of counseling but he or she may then face obstacles in making a referral. Each of the disciplines practising counseling has different training programs, and there are also huge differences within the disciplines. The most obvious differences between disciplines are the lengths of training programs, and whether or not an undergraduate degree or diploma are prerequisites before embarking on a professional qualification.

Clinical and counseling psychologists hold undergraduate degrees in psychology before completing three years of full-time training. Social workers hold either diplomas or undergraduate degrees before completing two years of full-time training.

Psychotherapists may or may not hold undergraduate degrees before completing three or four years full-time training. There is no consistency between psychotherapy training programs so each one has to be evaluated and understood in its own right. Some attract people who already have qualified as clinical psychologists, psychiatrists, counselors, and social workers. Others tend to attract people new to the field without undergraduate degrees or diplomas.

Counselors obtain diplomas in two years and many hold an undergraduate degree or diploma although it is not a requirement at all institutions. Like psychotherapy training institutes, each counseling institute needs to be evaluated and understood in its own right.

Public Services or the Private Sector?

The GP will have to consider public services and the private sector taking into account the patient's preference. In terms of the *National Health,* it is likely that the patient will have to wait six months for an appointment with a clinical psychologist. The GP may have a clinical or counseling psychologist, or counselor, or a community psychiatric nurse (CPN) attached to the practice in which case the referral will be simple.

It is becoming prevalent for GPs to have counselors on site in the practice. Some of these counselors are adequately qualified, while others are not. They include clinical and counseling psychologists, counselors with diplomas, counselors without diplomas, and community psychiatric nurses who may or may not have received counseling training.

Many counselors in GP practices are not properly qualified. Some GPs do not take counseling seriously enough to appreciate the responsibility involved in facilitating our emotional growth. There are GPs who ask their practice nurses to see patients for counseling whether or not these nurses are qualified counselors.

Thus it can be seen that there are GP surgeries where more and more practice nurses and counselors are being employed, many of whom are not adequately qualified. That is a big worry for the clinical and counseling psychology professions. Clinical and counseling psychologists, like myself, are only occasionally being employed in GP surgeries because we are more expensive than qualified and unqualified counselors. Family Health Service Authorities frequently take the cheap option, and then their patients do not get the quality of service they might expect. The very people we hope will be able to understand what we're going through - that is, health and mental health professionals are often unable to facilitate their clients' emotional processes because of insufficient counseling training, if any.

This fact seems to constitute a contradiction between the public's expectations and reality.

Social work is another option. The GP may refer the client through social services, again possibly having to face a lengthy waiting list. Another possibility is psychiatry. Past experience may well have shown that psychiatrists are more likely to offer medication than emotional growth, and often the two do seem to be polar opposites. Occupational therapists and physiotherapists working with severely emotionally distressed clients in psychiatric units rarely have a counseling diploma. This often leaves health professionals feeling disillusioned and undervalued.

There is yet another separate discipline called "psychotherapy." You may say to yourself, "How can this be? I thought clinical psychologists and counselors practised psychotherapy." You're absolutely right, of course. But I write about the way we British organize professional groups who practise counseling and psychotherapy, and in this instance we do it quite differently from the rest of the world, probably because the British love to put people in classes. Social class permeates the culture and some of those supposed to be promoting mental health seem to automatically introduce arbitrary distinctions between groups with a wish to convey some sense of elitism.

There are further complications with the descriptors used by mental health professionals. Often the "psychotherapist" turns out to be a medical student or a newly qualified psychiatrist, with no training in psychotherapy or counseling, whose work will be supervised by a psychiatrist or clinical psychologist who has done some psychotherapy training. Clients attending these psychotherapy sessions often believe that they are receiving the best treatment reserved for the elite. They are not routinely informed that the psychiatrist practising psychotherapy has no qualifications at all in that particular area.

These terms are unfortunately heavily loaded politically within the professional groups, making it nigh on impossible for non-counselors to discover who's who and what's what in the field of "mental health," or "mental illness", depending upon one's perspective of the way these groups compete. The real losers resulting from this infantile competition, are members of the general public requiring responsive, helpful, and understandable services.

Another possible route is the student counselor. Carl Rogers developed his client-centered approach, later called person-centered, in university settings. American universities have large counseling centers and the students are encouraged to make good use of them. When students convey to academic advisers that they are having relationship problems or that their feelings are in some way preventing them from getting on with their college work, most advisers will suggest, in a low-key way, that perhaps it would be helpful to make an appointment over at the Counseling Center. The attitude is that all proper preventive measures should take place so that students can address any emotional issues sooner rather than later. Perhaps this is where the myth comes from that every American has his or her own analyst. While that is absolutely false, it is true that many Americans have, at least, some first-hand experience of therapy or counseling. Not so, relatively speaking, for the British. What most British people know about counseling comes from novels, movies, friends or relatives.

In our universities we also have counselors, but very few on any given campus. British students often only get referred to a campus counselor when their emotional difficulties have become full-blown. It is as if the idea of counseling is an after-thought, or perhaps a last resort, to the British. Very often, the referral is made too late to prevent a suicide, or full blown alcohol or drug-related problem. What is this prejudice in our society about working on our emotional health? As with most prejudices, its irrationality produces much unnecessary pain and distress. It sometimes results in an inability to function.

Another significant difference between British and American student counselors is that American student counselors usually hold a doctorate in either counseling or clinical psychology, while British student counselors usually have a counseling diploma. Again, it seems that the Americans take counseling more seriously than the British. On an American university campus, the counseling clinic may employ twenty full-time counselors. In British universities, there may be only two or three working part-time.

Although it is not possible to comment on all the public health settings where clients and counselors can be found, I will nevertheless attempt to mention enough of them to demonstrate how widely spread the practice of counseling is, and how little attention is paid as to whether or not the "counselors" have any qualifications relevant to the responsibilities involved in the work. For example, counselors specialize in bereavement counseling. *Bereavement counselors* who go to people's homes with the label "trained counselor" may have completed a six week course in counseling. Others have trained for a year.

Specialist nurses counseling people with chronic and terminal illnesses have often only had similar brief exposure to counseling training. *Rape crisis centers* and *women's refuge centers* employ counselors who may or may not have a recognized qualification. Numerous support groups are operational for victims of brutality by qualified and unqualified group psychotherapists.

Large numbers of counselors, qualified and unqualified, are employed to work with t*he homeless, the unemployed, the elderly in residential settings,* and *the young in job training schemes.* These examples are consistent with the frightening issue here. A large number of counselors have no qualifications for the work they do with people's emotional health and mental illness. People are expected to learn by trial and error on the job with very little supervision, or are sent on some short counseling skills courses to help them along.

Some of the unqualified counselors referred to above come on my five-day counseling skills courses. They often seem to be experiencing high levels of stress in their work. The frustrations have to do with the lack of supervision, training, and support. There also seems to be considerable guilt about working with populations at an emotional level for which they are unqualified. This results in people taking home with them the worries about how they handled situations with clients, without a very constructive way of working through their concerns.

Remember, for the most part, people working as counselors with clients in extreme emotional distress and often without social support, have probably not done exploratory work on themselves, nor have they taken full courses in psychology or counseling. Their training needs are expected to be met simply with five-day intensive counseling skills courses. This situation is not good for any one and certainly is not promoting the mental health of staff or clients. Counselors in these situations often resort to befriending the clients because they lack counseling skills. Befriending, as a part of the counseling relationship, is of course contrary to the British Association for Counselling's ethical code. There is a great deal of confusion here about the way various agencies operate. This deplorable situation exists because clients who could benefit from counseling have no easy access to counselors and psychotherapists. In fact, it sometimes seems as if those clients who are most desirous of therapy are denied it and fobbed off with befrienders. It really is not fair.

I have described the difficulties involved in making choices from public services. Finding one's way around the *private sector* for fee-paying services is not so straightforward either. If the patient requests a private practitioner, the GP may consider a referral to a clinical psychologist. Depending upon whether the GP is used to making private referrals, he or she may have some particular psychologist in mind. However, there are GPs who prefer not to use private practitioners, sometimes because of their political views, in which case they may not assist their patients at all in that regard.

If the GP happens to already know of some counselors, the patient may well be referred in that direction. Most GPs are used to referring their patients to Relate, a national agency with high street branches, who implement a sliding scale. Some areas have local Counseling Centers which also operate sliding scales. Few GPs probably direct their patients to the *Directory of the British Association for Counselling* which lists qualified counselors, including information about their qualifications, approach to counseling, and fee structure.

The GP may know some social workers and family therapists who practise privately and may refer their patients on to them. Private referrals to psychiatrists may be made at the patients' requests. There are still those who assume that the most expert provider of mental health is the psychiatrist, associating a medical background with cure. Only a small proportion of psychiatrists are trained counselors so those patients often end up with rather expensive supportive psychotherapy which is separate from emotional growth. It is more akin to the "reassurance" health professionals sometimes resort to when they are feeling inadequate in terms of responding to the emotional health needs of their patients. As previously stated, these patients are just as likely to be medicated. It is important to state that there are, of course, many psychiatrists who are responsible enough in those situations to refer their patients on to qualified counselors, clinical and counseling psychologists, or psychotherapists.

Referral might be made directly to a psychotherapist in the private sector and the GP would then have to choose between a psychoanalyst or psychoanalytic psychotherapist (Freudian, Kleinian, Independent, Lacanian or Jungian), a behavioral psychotherapist (radical or cognitive), family psychotherapist (systemic or structural), hypnotherapist, neurolinguistic programming therapist, person-centered, Gestalt, Adlerian, or a transactional analysis therapist, to name but a few. How many GPs really understand the differences between all of these approaches?

Hardly any. Many tend to refer to psychotherapists whose work is familiar to them, regardless of the therapist's orientation. Basically, if a therapist has helped patients in the past, more referrals are made in the future. If

GPs get to know a few psychotherapists with differing orientations, then they may discover over time that one approach seems to suit some sorts of emotional issues better than others, so they can make educated referrals based on past experience with a tiny sample of psychotherapists or counselors. Going to a private practitioner requires just as much care as seeing someone in the public services. Often, practitioners like myself work in both the public and private sectors.

At a deeper level, a painful chord strikes when these situations are explored having to do with the fact that health professionals are also sometimes patients, and we may face our own fears of being treated by unqualified counselors in our time of need. We expect people who carry out health procedures on our body to be well-qualified. Why should we expect less from anyone who has access to our emotional health? When are we going to take ourselves seriously and experience each other as unique individuals requiring, at times, specialized care for our minds as well as our bodies?

Assessment, Facilitation or Both?

Each client has his or her own characteristic way of beginning relationships. From the first point of contact, both the counselor and client are processing impressions of each other. The client may very well have formed impressions of the therapist prior to that point, in anticipation of the consultation. The counselor needs to ward off the impulse of anticipating what the client will be like, because it is important to meet each client with an open mind, rather than with a fixed set of expectations.

The initial session may begin with the counselor indicating the duration of the session (perhaps an hour), making it clear that it is for the client to use the time as he or she thinks best. Sometimes a simple, "How can I be of help?" or "It's up to you," is enough to facilitate the client to begin.

Some clients speak for five minutes describing a crisis, or an onset of symptoms such as panic attacks, and having described what's going on, look at the counselor expectantly for a reaction and perhaps even a magic cure. This moment is crucial in setting the stage for what counseling entails. The counselor acknowledges what the client has so far described and perhaps also lets the client know how he or she seemed to feel about the situation. For example, "You've told me what happened last week when you were out with your friends, about suddenly feeling overwhelmed with anxiety for no apparent reason, and how frightening that was for you."

Clients usually continue once the confirmation has been received from the counselor that what is being communicated is being heard. Then they are able to tell more about themselves in their individual ways, rather than being directed with questions. There is no saying in what direction the client will take the session. The counselor's job is to closely follow the client's process by listening and attending to both verbal and nonverbal communications. It is important to be able to assess whether or not psychotherapeutic input may be of help at the present time. In order to make that assessment, the counselor needs to facilitate the client's expression of his or her emotional life.

Directive counselors are more likely to follow a question-answer format in the initial session. Their aim is to identify with clients the main problems and to think of ways to overcome them. The reason I am opposed to that approach has to do with the fact that it prevents the client from saying what he or she may have said in the initial session. In other words, the agenda gets set by the counselor rather than the client. The opportunity may be lost for ever for the client to express deeper parts of himself or herself which were accessible at the time. Deeper issues may get pushed back and forgotten as the directive counselor continues to interrogate the client.

When I began practising psychotherapy in the UK, colleagues were surprised that my assessments of clients were not formal history-taking sessions. I was not prepared to behave one way with a client in the initial session, asking loads of questions, and then to take on a nondirective stance in subsequent sessions. That would give the client a double message. First the counselor would be saying, "What *I* want to ask you about is the important thing today." In ensuing sessions, the message would be, "*You* take the lead now." Let's be honest with our clients and let them explore themselves in their own ways, free to project on to us ideas, feelings, and conflicts that they bring from significant relationships.

First Things First

The most important observations that need to be made in the first session are how the client enters into a relationship. We all have characteristic ways of interacting, even when we are on our best behavior. It is not true that people act with therapists so differently from the way they are with other people in their lives, that we do not see them as they truly are.

Think about some of the most acclaimed actors. No matter what role they play, we discover consistent aspects of their personalities that cannot be removed. For example, actors move in their own characteristic way (unless the character is so different from themselves that the acting requires them to move differently). Often they play people of their own age and background. Their voices remain the same, so that idiosyncratic vocal inflections can be heard that stem from their own personalities. My point is that most of our clients do not have the acting talent of Meryl Streep and even if they wanted to could not behave completely differently from how they usually do with any consistency.

It is important to recognize the importance of remaining neutral and anonymous enough in the initial session to see how the client behaves without too much distraction from the counselor. Some clients sit on the edge of their seats with a fixed gaze on the counselor, and perhaps lots of smiles too in an attempt to win him or her over. Others sit as far back as possible, behaving as if the counselor is not present. When faced with these two extremes, I begin to put together a hypothetical picture of someone who has an overdriven need to be liked and who uses relationships as a way of seeing himself or herself reflected back in the reassuring and loving expressions of those with them. Such people often have low self-esteem and a dread of introspection because of feeling empty and desolate inside. In contrast, I would hypothesize that the client who begins the relationship as though the counselor does not exist, avoids entering into most relationships because of difficulties in getting close to people due to shyness, fear or hostility.

It is inevitable that other relational issues will emerge revealing what the person is like in significant relationships. The counselor and client will need to work out appointment times, payment of fees and various other practicalities. The ease or discomfort which the client demonstrates in these negotiations may indicate how he or she typically responds to potential conflict.

For example, some people are completely agreeable to the first options presented in terms of times and fee. Others react in a resigned but resentful way, and there are those who have huge difficulties agreeing either times or fees, because of some overdriven need to have special allowances made for them. I am not saying that any one of these styles is better or worse than any other.

There is no correct way to be. But the way the client begins the relationship does illustrate how the client responds to daily demands in life and allows a picture to be pieced together of the person gradually, not only based on what he or she reports is going on, but what we see goes on before us without enquiring at all. It is so important to use these observations to the client's advantage.

The counselor has to keep up with what is being said, how the client is entering into this new relationship, and what his or her life has been like. The best way of understanding is to be with the client in the session attending to all of these aspects, and distracting him or her as little as possible. The session is for the client. Our job is to protect that space, to facilitate a self-exploratory experience. Notice it is not our experience I want clients to get in touch with, but theirs.

The Past is Important

Person-centered therapy is not a diagnostic approach. Psychoanalytic psychotherapy usually is. The only problem I have with diagnosis is when it is used to classify people rather than getting to know them as unique human beings.

Over the last twelve years, working in London, I have been concerned about inadequate assessments that are routinely made of clients. There are humanistic counselors who stay far away from clients' early lives, to the point of not knowing what kind of surroundings they grew up in, birth order, number of siblings, nor attitudes towards significant people early on in their lives. These counselors reject any way of working that resembles psychoanalysis and consider it much more helpful to focus only on the present.

It is possible for clients to provide this information without the session turning into an interrogation. Usually most of it is provided spontaneously without any questions at all. It may become necessary towards the end of a session, or even in a subsequent session to make some enquiries, in order to have some sense of what our clients' lives have been like. I have never been able to work effectively with clients, either directly or indirectly, as the therapist, or the counselor's supervisor, without having the client's report of what they can remember about the way they felt early on in life. If the goal of psychotherapy and counseling is for the person to feel more integrated, their early life cannot be split off from the present. I am not suggesting that we teach people to dwell negatively on difficulties that may have existed in the past. What I suggest is that people more readily acknowledge that the way they respond to important events that are happening now, has a great deal to do with how they felt about major events early on in life, and how the significant people in their lives interpreted and responded to those events.

By ignoring the past, we are not able to creatively integrate it into the present. In fact, clients go round and round in circles along with their counselors when both of them refuse to acknowledge the client's whole experience of living. It is important to know, for example, to whom the client was closest as far back as he or she remembers. Most people say there was no difference, having been brought up to believe that members of families all love each other the same, meaning in equal amounts, I presume. How many of us have heard parents say, "I love all my children the same."? I experience that phrase initially as a declaration of insanity, but when I regain my own sanity I appreciate that it is simply part and parcel of society's ignorance about emotional life.

To whom was the client closest? I want to know whether the client trusted a mother figure or a father figure more than the other. It helps me understand better what is going on in current relationships with men and women, because I believe those early feelings are carried over to the present. To help the client explore this question, I often add, "Who did you tell if something happened at school, like if you got hurt, or if you did well?" That often produces a response which may be helpful in putting together a picture of who the person is. It enables the client to give examples of how he or she interacted with significant others early on in life.

I also want to know the **birth order of siblings** including those who did not survive. **How old was my client when the next child was on its way?** For example, for how long did the client experience being the youngest, and all that went along with that? It is not the same for everyone? What was it like for the client? There may not be an actual memory of it, but associated ideas and feelings will be helpful in filling in the picture of who the client is.

Who else lived at home when my client was growing up? The significant other may have been a grandparent, uncle, aunt or lodger. He or she may no longer be in the client's awareness, and unless the client is specifically asked if there were others living at home than those immediately mentioned, a very important part of the picture may be missing. In other words, the most significant people in a person's life are not always mothers, fathers, or siblings. For each family unit it can vary.

What was it like growing up in my client's family environment? What did the adults do occupationally, for leisure and for holidays? In which groups did they have membership - religious, political, sports, pubs, clubs, educational, or were they loners? **What were their personalities like - the adults' and the children's? Who was my client most like in terms of personality? With whom was there most conflict, and with whom most trust?** I begin to get a sense of who my client is as I listen to the free associations in response to these enquiries; and I see if and where these relationships get replayed in my client's life, as well as in my consulting room; and I share my observations with my client when there is enough evidence for them to be meaningful. Some clients are unable to respond to these enquiries, unable to remember how they felt. Then we can only work with the present and recent past.

I particularly want to know **whether the client has seen a counselor or therapist before**. This information often does not emerge for a long time unless it is specifically requested. I find it useful to know how the client felt about previous therapy sessions. I want to know whether or not therapy was helpful.

If it was helpful, how was it helpful? This enables me to more quickly comprehend what the client experiences as helpful. It provides some indication of whether or not the client will experience my approach as helpful, and it allows me the opportunity of advising the client, if it seems important at the time to do so, of the similarities and differences that are likely to be present here. It may be unnecessary to burden the client with all of this information, but it is useful for the therapist to understand as much as possible about the client's frame of reference.

For example, if a client told me that she had seven previous therapists and none of them understood her, I would probably not be optimistic that she will experience me as helpful. Should a client indicate that he had seven previous therapists who were all very helpful, I would be wondering out loud how come he is now beginning therapy with me. I would not be optimistic that the therapy would be helpful. In other words, the answers to the questions about previous therapy only add to the details that begin to portray the person. The answers are not useful if used too concretely. Nevertheless, once I know something of the attitude to the psychotherapy process, I can communicate with a client about it from his or her perspective, rather than mine.

Back to the Present

Before the session is over, it is usually necessary for me to bring the client back to the present, so that we can reconsider the detailed symptoms described at the beginning of the session. We can begin to hypothesize about the meaning of the symptoms in light of the increased information now available about the client's past and present. In that sense, we have come full circle from first observing and experiencing how the client began the psychotherapy relationship, and then hearing his or her account of some past memories, and finally bringing the client back to the present, so that we can facilitate movement towards integration.

The dialogue below exemplifies the way initial sessions can begin:

*CLIENT: *I've been feeling anxious now for some time. Some days I don't make it to work, because when I start to get ready to leave home I suddenly break out in a sweat. My whole body starts trembling and I feel overwhelmed, I can't explain it, but it's like some unexplainable fear. It is so scary. This must sound. . . so . . . I'm sorry. I really shouldn't have come. I can't explain it.*

THERAPIST: *It sounds like it's hard for you to talk about the scary feelings you've been having, because you don't understand them and you're worried about trying to describe them to me, a total stranger.*

CLIENT: *When I start trembling, I have this feeling . . . I know this sounds weird . . . but I have this feeling that something terrible is about to happen. My doctor gave me betablockers and I suppose that should solve the problem, but lately it's got so bad, my work is not like it should be.*

THERAPIST: *You've described some of the distressing symptoms you've been experiencing recently. What would also be helpful is if you could tell me more about yourself, so that I can begin to get a sense of who you are and what your life is like, has been like, and your hopes for the future?*

CLIENT: *Well, I'm not sure what it is you want to know. You want to know about my life. I've just had an ordinary life. I don't know why this is happening to me. You want to know about my life? you mean, like my wife and family. Well, we're having some problems, but I don't know if I should talk about that, if it's relevant? Or my past? I really don't know what to say.*

THERAPIST: *Take your time. Go with whatever comes to mind.*

In terms of the present, by the end of a session where I have listened carefully and not asked many questions, I would expect to have some idea of who the important characters are in the client's life now, the client's living arrangement (whether he or she lives alone or with a partner, family,

---

*All of the vignettes in this book are fictitious. None of them are taken from any particular sessions with any of my clients. They do, however, convey they way some of us speak as clients and therapists.

or friends), who provides most support and what triggers off most anxiety or tension.

Ending the Initial Session

Another question I have in mind throughout the session which the client will need me to answer is, **"Will psychotherapy with you as my therapist help, and if so, how?"** I may find that the client has no inclination to self-explore and only wants symptom relief. In that case, I will tell the client that my impression is that nothing short of symptom relief is likely to satisfy him or her, and with my approach symptom relief may take some months. The client then has the choice to work with me at least for a few months or to seek out a behavioral approach which may bring about speedy symptom relief for the time being.

It is important that counselors and psychotherapists accept responsibility to inform clients that there are alternative therapists to themselves. In that way I acknowledge that I am not going to be the best therapist for most people. However, I might be the best that is available, and I will probably be good enough. What is all this business about responsibility? If I go to a store to buy a sweater, I do not expect the salesperson to tell me three other places to buy alternative types of merchandise. However, the sweater is not going to affect the shopper in the same way as the therapy might. Psychotherapy calls for a client to trust the discretion of the therapist. It is only to the extent that the client can trust the therapist, in terms of being a responsible, ethical and clinically qualified professional that the client can risk telling the therapist about himself or herself without fear of ridicule, judgment or exploitation.

If clients do seem ready to self-explore, I have to consider warning them about the process sometimes being slow and painful, as well as solid and in the long-term rewarding. Also, some explanation about the transferential nature of the relationship may be forthcoming. Clients often appreciate being told at the outset that they can expect to experience a whole range of feelings towards me. In fact, we can anticipate that at times feelings they have experienced in their lives towards significant people in their lives, may be felt about me, and our job in therapy will be to take hold of these feelings, to understand them, and to better appreciate both their origin and meaning. I explain to them that the value of the psychotherapy relationship is that we can do that here as part of the work, and use those feelings as they emerge for the client's increased self-understanding.

By the end of the initial session, I expect to have an informed opinion as to whether or not the client has some likelihood of benefiting from psychotherapy, and specifically in what ways. It is in the last fifteen or twenty minutes of the initial session, usually, that I tell the client that I want to say how I have received his or her communications in terms of the various issues that seem to be important at the moment. I often say that I need to hear from the client, first, as to whether or not I seem to be on the right track, and to hear the client's reaction to the idea of embarking on a psychotherapy relationship.

Until the client has had a chance to explore out loud whether or not ongoing psychotherapy might be considered, I cannot come to an opinion as to the benefits of psychotherapy for him or her. There are a number of possible consequences of having directed clients, in the initial session, to consider the *pros* and *cons* of psychotherapy, either with me or someone else of a similar or quite different orientation. The first possible consequence is that clients will either indicate that my initial impressions seemed to sum up what they wanted to convey, or that I seem to have misunderstood, or they will express uncertainty as to whether I understood or not.

If the client felt well understood at the end of the first session, we could go on to consider the possible benefits and disadvantages of continuing with psychotherapy. In the event that the client felt misunderstood, it may be unrealistic to expect the client to reach any immediate decision. I then offer another appointment in case clients want time between sessions to see how they felt about the initial session, or they sometimes wish to return to see if they feel any better understood next time. I encourage dissatisfied clients to let me direct them to various other therapists and services, making it clear that therapists differ in their approaches. When clients felt uncertain about the first session, I offered them the same options as to those who felt completely misunderstood.

I want to make it clear at the outset that the last part of the initial session is *a collaborative effort* on the part of the client and therapist to reach some mutual agreement as to how to proceed and for what purpose. I take the responsibility to lead the client into a relationship with me which has the potential of becoming a working or therapeutic alliance. The truly person-centered position would be to refrain from that directive. I, however, wish to show how I work. This is a crucial intervention on my part which sends a powerful message to the client.

over

The message is that I have a responsibility to provide a service and I am imposing on him or her, with subtle pressure, my need for that responsibility to be shared so that we can work together.

Contradictions between Assessment and Facilitation

I have been advocating the need to know something of the client's initial relationships and experiences of the world. I have also been stressing the importance of maintaining a nondirective stance. Usually it is not possible to achieve both.

In my beginning years as a therapist, I sacrificed information so as to remain nondirective. I think I was right. That was the only way I could learn to be truly nondirective. However, it may not have been very helpful for my clients. I would do the same again. I believe that once I was experienced in my work, clients benefited because I had persevered as a nondirective therapist. Later on when I did mix my interventions by occasionally becoming directive, I was entirely aware of the switch and ready to accept that I was taking the client off track in order to obtain some background material that might speed up our understanding of his or her emotional process.

What feels risky to me about putting this process into words, is that it could encourage less experienced counselors to become directive too soon. Not only that, but perhaps it is possible for some nondirective counselors to maintain that stance and still get plenty of background material without directing the client at all. That would be the ideal situation as far as I am concerned.

I think it is important for counselors to have enough information to formulate some working hypotheses which they share with clients, so that both of them can feel that they are working together, sooner rather than later. Certainly, that can wait until the last part of the initial session so that the clients at least have thirty-five minutes to express themselves in their own ways. The first thirty-five minutes may be the only time in the therapeutic relationship which is truly nondirective. Once we have directed them, they begin to make their own hypotheses, usually unconsciously, of what we need to hear and how best to gratify or deprive us and the relationship.

To Conclude

Clients need to tell us about themselves as freely as possible in the initial session. What they push back in that session is unlikely to ever come up again with that counselor or therapist. The unconscious decision may have already been made that the counselor cannot be trusted with particular feelings, ideas, or memories. Most people do not give us a second chance, because the initial decision results in instant repression and the path is set with some immediacy for the kind of therapeutic experience that will follow.

The reality is that no one would be able to work with all of a client's feelings and memories. No matter how nondirective or nonjudgmental the counselor is there will always be limitations on how much one person can facilitate a client's emotional and personal growth. Each of us acquires our own ways of intervening and being with people in therapeutic relationships. My hope is that at least each therapist has a sense of how his or her way of working at times is facilitative, and how it can sometimes be experienced as prohibitive.

CHAPTER
S I X

Emotions, and the way we feel about them

WELLWISHER: *How are you?*

CARER: *Fine, how are you?*

WELLWISHER: *Oh, I'm fine. I was concerned about you now that your husband's mobility has deteriorated. How are you feeling?*

CARER: *We'll get through. It is hard, but there's no use in complaining about it, is there?*

WELLWISHER: *No, I guess not, but let me know if I can help.*

CARER: *Thanks. I appreciate your concern.*

The dialogue above demonstrates a wellwisher who was trying to get in touch with a carer's feelings. The carer was unable to respond at a feeling level, leaving the wellwisher only with the option of offering her help. In other words, while he was interested in her feelings, the subject matter of the interaction rapidly reverted to practicalities.

The Uniqueness of Experiencing Beings

What makes it so difficult for us to communicate at a more emotional level? Perhaps it has to do with the fact that each of us is *unique* and it is difficult to appreciate what effect a traumatic event has on a particular person. The carer was traumatized because of the loss of her husband's mobility and the radical changes that had made in their lives. Neither she nor the wellwisher was aware initially of how she felt about it, because feelings tend to emerge gradually, rather than thoughts which are instant.

That example allows us, perhaps, to better understand the complexities involved in getting in touch with our emotional lives. In humanistic psychology, people are viewed as *experiencing beings*. Experiencing suggests that we are in some sort of process. The carer is in the process of taking in some new harsh reality, in terms of her husband's disability. From moment to moment she will have a variety of feelings because they are not static.

Often when wondering what another person is experiencing, people get stuck. Experience is not only to do with events that have occurred in an individual's life, but how those events have been perceived. Each of us is born into our own inner world which contains its own significant characters, who can provide and deprive. Early on, an imprint is made on the individual, as to the way the world is. It then becomes necessary to integrate that inner world with the outer world and in some way to reconcile them. It becomes evident why it is so difficult to understand what another person is going through when our individual experiences of the 'worlds' in which we live differ so much one from the other.

When I meet with a new client, an *experiencing being,* how can I know what his or her world is like? I listen. I wait. I facilitate the client's process. I am aware that I can only know a fraction of his or her experience at any given moment in time, which prepares me well to journey along in a nondirective way so that together we can discover more about the client's emotional life.

I take a *holistic* view, so that I am aware that along with an emotional process goes a physiological one. When I work with clients, I am aware that their experience includes what is going on in their body at any moment in time, and that there are ongoing physiological sensations occurring simultaneously along with emotional ones. I try to keep in mind the whole person.

Each of us is *unique*. Therefore, it is important to remember that what may appear to be an identical experience will be *experienced* in different ways by each person. Events are experienced in the context of a person's whole life. For example, a woman who became managing director of a public company may have consistently achieved the best results as a schoolchild, teenager and young adult in everything she did; or, on the other hand, she may not have been particularly successful as a child. She may have been someone who endeavored to achieve, but usually her attempts were met with disappointment. Clearly, the feelings about her appointment as managing director would differ depending on past experience.

The above example seems so obvious. Yet, it is fair to say that there is a tendency to assume how someone feels when they tell us what we interpret as 'good news', as we do when we believe we have been told 'bad news'. There is no room for assumptions if we are to facilitate our clients' emotional growth. Assumptions are set aside once an empathic stance is adopted in nondirective counseling and psychotherapy.

Not knowing is my state of mind when I listen most effectively to my clients. Being aware that my clients know far more about themselves, their lives, the important people in their lives and indeed all of their circumstances, creates an atmosphere where I feel somewhat *in awe* of them. This feeling results in a deeply felt wish to be of help without intruding, invading, or even inadvertently insulting them.

I know nothing about my clients. They begin to make themselves known to me in their own ways. If I can keep in mind the enormity of what it would be to know all of their experience, then I can maintain my sense of not knowing, but wanting to know. And I remain in awe of them as I begin to discover who they are, accompanying them on their journey to learn more about themselves.

I have a tremendous amount of catching up to do, and no time to assume anything. For me, that is what makes the task such an adventure. It is not possible to predict what someone else's life has been like, even if they grew up next door and had membership in the same groups as we did. Most of us do not know very much about the inner experiences of the people closest to us - that is, parents, siblings, other relatives and friends. To make assumptions about clients based on a referral letter is, of course, a nonsense. I vote for *not knowing* as the most helpful position.

Some Background on Needs, Motivation, Conflict Resolution, Tension Reduction and Self-Actualization

Each of us has biological and emotional needs. Some of these get met some of the time. In the process we experience frustration, tension, and conflict which we strive to tolerate, reduce and resolve. The ways we choose largely depend on our personalities. There are numerous theories of personality and each one seeks to understand what motivates various human reactions, such as behavior, feelings, attitudes and thought. Some basic concepts derived from psychoanalytic and humanistic schools of psychology follow. I have selected those that are most meaningful to me in my day-to-day work as a psychotherapist.

Sigmund Freud (1856-1939)

Freud (1923) conceptualized personality as being comprised of three structural components - *id*, *ego* and *superego*. These terms were metaphors to enable us to consider mental contents and processes in a particular way. He described the *id* as the structure seeking satisfaction of the individual organism's innate needs. "It is the ego's task to meet the demands raised by its three dependent relations - to reality, to the id, and to the superego - and nevertheless at the same time to preserve its own organization and maintain its own autonomy. The severest demand on the ego is probably the keeping down of the instinctual claims of the id, to accomplish which it is obliged to maintain large expenditures of energy . . . An action by the ego is as it should be if it satisfies simultaneously the demands of the id, of the superego, and of reality - that is to say, if it is able to reconcile their demands with one another. . . The superego's main function remains the limitation of satisfactions . . . "(Freud, 1949).

The *ego* acts as a mediator and not only has to decide if demands can be met, but also has to exercise judgment as to when the circumstances in the external world are most favorable. At other times, the *ego* decides that the need cannot be met, so that it must be suppressed, "but the demands made by the superego too may become so powerful and so relentless that the ego may be paralyzed, as it were, in the face of its other tasks. The id and the superego often make common cause against the hard-pressed ego which tries to cling to reality in order to retain its normal state. If the other two become too strong, they succeed in loosening and altering the ego's organization, so that its proper relation to reality is disturbed or even brought to an end." Considerable tension can be produced in this process, which is generally felt as 'unpleasure,' (too much tension), while the lowering of tension is experienced as 'pleasure'. The ego strives after pleasure, the lowering of tension, and seeks to avoid unpleasure, too much tension (Freud, 1949).

Freud (1949) posited the existence of sexual and aggressive drives which combine and make up the instinctual aspects of mental life. The two basic instincts, *Eros* and *Thanatos*, are biological functions, which operate against each other or combine with each other. He gave the example of the act of eating as a destruction of the object with the final aim of incorporating it, and the sexual act as an act of aggression with the purpose of the most intimate union. The libido is the total available energy of *Eros*, the erotic drive, and the libido neutralizes the destructive tendencies which are simultaneously present.

Psychoanalysis and other methods of self-exploration enable people to recognize how they have typically responded to different types of conflicts in the past, and allows them the opportunity to change in the future, to develop ways of tolerating frustrations, reducing tension and resolving conflict coming from within or without.

Abraham Maslow (1908-1970)

Humanistic psychologists believe that people are motivated to move towards self-actualization which would be for the good of themselves as well as the good of the larger society. Deprivation of needs, as well as internal and external conflict sometimes get in the way, and stop people from fully realizing their true potential.

Maslow's needs hierarchy is particularly helpful in this regard. His ideas are based on his constructions of personality traits and characteristics which emerged from his clinical work. The hierarchy was made up of five levels: physiological, safety, love, esteem and self-actualization. People's basic needs have to be met, before they can move on to the next level. In other words, the need for food precedes needs for shelter, feeling loved and a sense of belonging, self-esteem, and the need to be altruistic (Maslow, 1970).

Moving from one level to the next is only possible if external and inner resources are available to act as motivators. In therapy the obstacles to moving on are identified and better understood. I use the model in a simple way. I assume that each of us is on a path moving towards health. That is the way people want to go. However, there are times, many times for most of us, when we get blocked along the path by some obstacle. In therapy, we can begin to identify the obstruction and learn more about it. What aspects of it have come perhaps from some inner conflict, and how has the external environment contributed to the impasse?

The answers to these questions are not so simple. It will take hard work in terms of a willingness to introspect and explore, to come up with some possible hypotheses. It may be that the obstruction is adaptive. Possibly, the person needed to take a breath, to stop, to review, and to consider, before moving on. Alternatively, the obstruction may be maladaptive, preventing him or her from reaching some higher level of self-fulfilment. Either way, the obstruction deserves some respect. It can symbolize some important meanings about the person and the stage he or she has reached or is moving toward in life. Moving up the needs hierarchy depends upon being able to use both inner and outer resources constructively, providing those resources are in good supply.

Carl R. Rogers (1902-1986)

By this time, you may be feeling somewhat anxious. I am. All this talk about needs and conflict can be upsetting. It is upsetting because most people do not like to think of themselves as needy or conflicted. They become anxious when their *self-concepts* are inconsistent with their ideal selves, and it is out of that mismatch between the way they believe themselves to be, as contrasted with the way they sometimes feel and behave that produces anxiety. That is Carl Rogers' way of understanding anxiety and it can be very helpful when working with clients who are at a loss to understand their uneasiness and distress (Rogers, 1957).

Anxiety

The way I try to understand people in distress is by applying Rogers' theory concerning self-concept *versus* experience, and the ensuing *incongruence*, which produces anxiety. I take his theory further and use it in a way that is consistent with the psychoanalytic notion of symptoms as compromise formations (Freud, 1966). Let the following example describe how these concepts get translated into practice:

> A woman, aged forty, and mother of eighteen year old son living at home with her in London, developed symptoms of tiredness, loss of appetite and generally felt lethargic. She was not psychologically sophisticated.

> Her son was due to leave home in two weeks' time to go to university. Since mother was psychologically unsophisticated she was not in touch with her deeper *self-concept*. Nevertheless, it was evident that she viewed herself as 'a good mother', and needed others also to view her that way.

> Her conscious experience of letting her son go was one of pride and hope for his wellbeing in the future. There was a feeling of satisfaction that he had achieved good enough exam results to get into college. At a deeper level, however, there was separation anxiety and all that goes along with that. The overall *experience* was mixed. At one level mother was very pleased with her son's development, but at a level so much

deeper that it was not in her awareness, there was considerable anxiety connected with the loss of her son as he moved toward adulthood, changing her role as a mother.

Mother was confronted with a mismatch between her self-concept and her experience. For her, a good mother was someone who would only feel joy, pride and happiness for a son moving on to complete his education and attain his independence; separation anxiety would be a selfish and inappropriate response. When anxiety inevitably began to emerge, even before it reached her awareness, it was automatically pushed back, because it was in conflict with her self-concept, and not allowed natural expression. The feelings produced *incongruence* between her self- concept - "I am a good mother", and her experience of dread at letting him go, so the unacceptable feelings were instantly converted into physiological symptoms, which was the only way they could be expressed without destroying her self-concept. Mother was now able to experience *anxiety* even though the true cause was masked. Her self-concept was in this way protected, because an ill mother can still be 'a good mother'.

The above example can be very helpful in understanding people in distress. It is also helpful in rectifying counseling sessions which seem stuck. Often clients talk about feeling generally anxious and at odds with themselves, and they hope that they will understand more once they have described the symptoms. There are times when the description does not seem to help, and both the counselor and client feel stuck, because neither of them are listening to the distress in the context of the client's self-concept.

To take the example further, let us consider how a GP (general practitioner or family doctor) could have been of most help with regard to the woman experiencing lethargy. Bear in mind, most patients are seen for five minute consultations by GPs in the UK. Once the GP was reasonably satisfied that there was no medical cause for the symptoms, he or she could enquire as to how things were generally.

PATIENT: *Things couldn't be better. My son is going off to college. We're so excited. I'm so proud of him. Everything in my life is fine. If only I didn't feel so weak. I feel ill most of the time.*

DOCTOR: *Will your son be living far away?*

PATIENT: *He has a place at Sussex. Not too far away.*

DOCTOR: *Sussex University? So this will be a big change for you, with your son moving on. I wonder how you are handling the separation anxiety.*

PATIENT: *Oh, come on doctor. He's not leaving the country. I'll hear from him frequently and he'll come home for some weekends. What do I have to feel anxious about? This is the happiest time of our lives.*

(At this point, it is evident that the patient is not tuned in at all to psychological processes. Let's hope her GP is!)

DOCTOR: *I can hear how happy you are about your son, and at the same time upset about not feeling well. I haven't found anything physical to explain your symptoms. All the tests fortunately have come back negative. I think you will feel better in no time, and I am here if you need me.*

In terms of the big change that is taking place in your life, as your doctor I need to give you some information. Separation anxiety is a set of feelings people experience whenever there is a big change in one's life. Letting go of a child, and all the ways you have looked after him from day to day will probably leave a void in your life until you adapt to the change. Allow yourself to be a bit unhappy about that for a while. Who wouldn't? It takes time to adapt to any change, no matter how good the change is. I think you may be feeling ill, because you cannot admit to yourself that you are a bit anxious about your future now that your life has changed.

PATIENT: *Well, if you haven't found anything wrong I suppose I should feel thankful. So there's no prescription?*

DOCTOR: *No. Give yourself some time and I'm sure you'll feel better. (Stands up). Come back in a few days and let me know how you are.*

PATIENT: *Thank you, doctor. Good-bye.*

DOCTOR: *Good-bye.*

I think this would have been the correct way to respond to the patient. The patient would probably have felt very disappointed with the doctor and may have considered the remarks about separation anxiety as a lot of nonsense. The most negative reaction would probably come out if a friend asked her what the doctor said about her lethargy.

PATIENT: *Doctors! Don't talk to me about doctors. He sounded more like a psychiatrist. He said all kinds of things about anxiety and feeling bad because I have to let go of my son. What a lot of nonsense. I've never been so thrilled in my life about him leaving home and going to college.*

FRIEND: *What did he say about the lethargy?*

PATIENT: *He said I should go back and see him in a few days. No prescription, nothing. Anxiety, that's all he talked about. Separation anxiety!*

The above response demonstrates the possible short-term effect of a holistic response to the patient. A few weeks later, when the woman may be feeling at quite a loss and not much better, she might remember what her doctor said to her. She may be able to recognize that indeed her life has changed now, and perhaps her symptoms were in some way symbolizing some aspect of all of that. The gradual recognition can result in a growing awareness that one can find it painful to let go of a son, and nevertheless still be a good mother.

An important point that becomes clear from the above has to do with the fact that correct responses to psychological processes rarely provide instant relief. They usually take time to process, to work through. However, the long term effect of correct responses can lead to emotional growth and deeper recognition of inner conflicts, wishes and feelings. That is why so many health professionals are unable to learn ways of being with their patients' psychological processes without proper training. What doctors, nurses and physiotherapists like best is client's satisfaction. Rarely will client satisfaction be present when people are attending to painful feelings. The benefits of emotional growth work are for the long-term, not the short-term. By the time people have fully benefited from sensitive care, they are unlikely to be seeing the health professional regularly for the original symptoms.

The doctor who was not tuned in to psychological processes may have responded to the patient impatiently once he was satisfied there was no physical problem. He may have not recognized the significance of the fact that there was an imminent important life change. Although the doctor may have known the patient for years, it may not have occurred to him that her self-concept was very much tied up with being a good mother.

The doctor may have fobbed the patient off with betablockers or antidepressants, depending upon his mood, and whatever he was projecting on to his patient at the time, anxiety or depression. It would not have been based on good clinical judgment. No pills were warranted unless the doctor merely wanted to pacify the patient in the short-term.

A little bit of psychological knowledge, if only about something as important and obvious as separation anxiety, can go a long way in responding appropriately to patients' needs. By having in mind Rogers (1957), Maslow (1970), Freud (1966), or dozens of other major personality theorists (DiCaprio, 1974) people can receive good medical and psychological attention in a single consultation. The example above described the strength of one's self-concept and how a woman felt at odds with herself when there was incongruence between it and her experience. With this in mind, it makes good sense to have some ideas about clients' self-concepts, so that when both client and counselor feel stuck, the counselor can begin to hypothesize how clients may be experiencing themselves as behaving or feeling in conflict with their ideal selves.

To make this important point clear, imagine what it must be like to have as a deep self-concept the perception, "I am a fair person." People with this idea about themselves sometimes find it difficult to tolerate any unfairness. In an imperfect world, imperfect human beings are unlikely to be successful in going through their entire lives being fair. Imagine then what it must be like to hold this value so dear and to notice oneself acting unfairly. It is bound to happen. Situations often arise where people have to take the fairest option, knowing that neither option is fair.

The 'fair person' may be feeling terrible about that, but is unaware that feeling terrible is connected in any way to having been unfair, because he thought the issue had been resolved. After all, he had banished it from memory stamped, "Done." The client would then be left feeling out of sorts with no idea why he felt so bad, looking at numerous issues, in the counseling session, except for the most troublesome one which has been repressed. If the counselor was aware that seeing himself as a fair person was paramount to the client, it would not be difficult to consider the possibility that he was experiencing pain due to having denied and possibly distorted some event in order to protect his self-concept.

Conditions of Worth

Nelson-Jones (1982) surveyed person-centered theory in a way that was particularly helpful to me. In particular, the concept of conditions of worth was described as emanating from the *need for positive regard from others*, which is a learned need, a need which develops in early infancy. The original example used by Rogers (1951) described a child who was deriving pleasure from hitting his baby brother until he was faced with the negative parental reaction of anger and displeasure. His parents communicated to him that his behavior was bad and totally unacceptable. They let him know that he was not loveable while enjoying himself in that way.

The child was young enough not to have developed a moral conscience, so that he was only aware of how much fun he was having by letting out some playful, but nevertheless rough, aggression on the baby. His parents' reaction struck him as odd. They seemed to be changing the rules. His understanding of life was that he was supposed to have a good time and they were supposed to watch him in a loving way. Suddenly, the child was conditioned to place a negative value on an enjoyable experience. The conflict was that on the one hand he was really having great fun hitting his baby brother, but on the other hand he also derived much pleasure from his parents when they expressed their love and admiration for him. It became apparent that he could not get both of these needs met simultaneously. One of them had to go, and what Rogers (1951) clarified in his example was that the need for positive regard from significant others was likely to be the much stronger need.

Rogers (1951) used this example to differentiate between an individual's *organismic valuing process* and a second valuing process based on *conditions of worth*. The child had to somehow resolve the conflictual position in which he found himself. Although he did not yet have the linguistic ability, he still needed in some way to comprehend the experience. He may have *accurately* represented the experience in his own mind, or he may have *distorted* it.

The accurate and distorted representations of the experience would be respectively, as follows: "While I experience the behavior as satisfying, my parents experience it as unsatisfyng," or, "I perceive this behavior as unsatisfying." In the latter case, his values were based on others' evaluations rather than his own organismic valuing process, and therefore were rightly called, conditions of worth. What is being described here is consistent with the socialization process - the imposition of rules which cannot yet make sense because of the child's limited understanding of the social, cultural, traditional and religious values of the significant people in his life. In terms of a child's developing personality, it is noteworthy whether a particular child tends to perceive the experience accurately or to rapidly distort it.

Depression

Loss is the key trigger that sets off depression. Too much distortion and repression can ultimately result in cumulative feelings of loss, loss of part of one self. Had the child referred to in the previous example accurately represented his experience, inasmuch as he was thoroughly enjoying himself before he met with his parents' disapproval, there would still have been room to daydream about the forbidden pleasure. There is no law against cultivating an active fantasy life. In fact, daydreaming and fantasy are very important mental activities and contribute to the creativity of the total personality.

It seems to me that a child who repeatedly attempts to resolve conflict by distorting and denying his or her experience is on the way to losing a part of his or her self. By denying part of the self, creative resources are inevitably closed off too. The tendency to develop a self based primarily on the requirements of others, and eventually authority figures in general, can result in the individual developing into a rigid and restrained person who is prone to *depression*.

People who develop a personality style essentially to satisfy others' conditions often have control problems, which are expressed in terms of rigid self-control and lack of tolerance for those who are more relaxed about either exerting self-control or controlling others. The individual who lost touch with his or her true self in those early years may keep all the rules all of the time because of an unconscious fear that spontaneous behavior would result in all of the rules being broken in an uncontrolled way. In fact, even to fantasize or daydream about forbidden behavior is too risky, because the individual who distorts and denies cannot always differentiate between imagining a situation and engaging in it (Shapiro, 1965).

In later life, people who developed in a rigid way are prone to depression, particularly if and when they review their lives, and sense that something was missing. A painful awareness may begin to emerge of a lost part of self, and it may be possible in counseling or psychotherapy to gently enable clients to be reunited with those repressed parts of themselves which were unavailable during the developmental years. However, the realization itself can be so painful, people may not be able to tolerate the very strong feelings that can emerge which have been stifled for most of their lives.

There is a vast difference between 'feeling depressed' and experiencing a full-blown clinical depression. The latter is fortunately much rarer. Yet feeling depressed is part of the whole spectrum of feelings we all experience from time to time. It includes feelings of hopelessness, helplessness, and negative views of self, the future, and the world in which one lives (Beck, 1976). It is not, however, an emotion that must instantly be eradicated with antidepressant medication, even if that were possible. Like any other emotion, it is to be recognized, understood, and respected as conveying some valuable information about what is going on at the moment in both the individual's inner and outer worlds.

I have seen many clients who have reported that they have been taking prescribed antidepressants for years. I was rarely able to detect a clinical depression. These clients certainly did feel depressed, however. It seemed to me that being prescribed antidepressants in a way made them feel more depressed, because they were being treated as though they were emotionally unwell. Mostly, I have found that there were valid reasons for these clients to feel depressed, but they were not ill.

People go to their GPs to tell them they feel depressed often in the hope that someone will listen to them. Instead, prescriptions are frequently handed to them. The message is thus rapidly conveyed that there is something pathological about feeling depressed. Alternatively, a referral could be made for counseling or psychotherapy providing clients with the rightful opportunity to explore what is making them miserable right now.

It is important to remember the principal part *loss* plays in setting off and maintaining *depression*. The loss may be obvious and apparent, or it may be harder to identify. In psychiatric units often only the most obvious losses are identified by the staff, leaving patients feeling misunderstood and confused. It is not always easy to identify loss of self-esteem, feelings of inadequacy, feared loss of love of a real or imagined person, loss of sense of stability, loss of self-confidence, and nagging guilt feelings.

Much research has been done by all of the major schools of psychotherapy with a view to identifying common thoughts, feelings and beliefs people experience when they are depressed. The findings seem to have much in common, despite the differences in each school's theoretical underpinnings. That is why I believe it is imperative for health professionals to have an ample understanding of the various kinds of losses that can be experienced and identified. To this end, a workable psychological theory must be used intelligently and responsibly - be it psychoanalytic, humanistic, or behavioral.

Assertiveness, and how it contributes to personal growth

Assertive clients often had more self-knowledge and engaged in personal growth work earlier than non-assertive clients who waited until the panic attacks or depth of depression were severe before reluctantly making arrangements to be seen for psychotherapy. Marked cultural differences between the USA and UK became apparent to me over time, as I practised in Cleveland, Ohio, and Chicago in the USA in the 1970's and early 1980's, and in London since that time. Americans are more consumer-oriented than the British, and Americans learn early in life that they have the right to stand up for themselves. However, that is not to say that in general Americans are more assertive in all areas of their lives, for each of us is unique.

A lack of assertiveness seems to create emotional difficulties for a number of people that I see. The word 'assertive' was not widely used until fairly recently in the UK. It has been more widely used in the USA over a longer period.

While working as a clinical psychologist in the USA, I did not find it necessary to focus on that issue in its own right with my clients. In the UK I have become more directive, at times giving information to clients, and educating them about the meaning and importance of assertiveness, and distinguishing it from aggressive and passive styles of relating. I seem to spend a great deal of my time defining and describing assertiveness, because a lack of it seems to lend itself to developing psychological symptoms, which is different from suggesting it to be their cause.

An *assertive* style of relating is entirely consistent with Rogers' notion of congruence. For me, what both have in common is the feeling of being true to oneself. An assertive stance is honest, open and direct; one that recognizes simultaneously one's rights and one's responsibilities. Being assertive means making one's own position known, by communicating clearly with others, and having regard for one's own feelings as well as others; it also means respecting self and others, and seeking ways of negotiating that take into consideration one's own needs as well as the needs of others, and endeavoring to state clearly what one's objectives are without feeling obligated to justify them. Assertiveness has more to do with *what* is going on than why. There is no room for mind-reading when maintaining an assertive stance (Butler, 1992).

An *aggressive* style of relating is designed to put the other person down. An aggressive stance is pushy, offensive, domineering, rude, arrogant and sometimes violent. Being aggressive usually assumes a competitive position; the desperate need to win is spurred on by the individual's low self-esteem in an attempt to improve a poor self-image.

A *passive* style of relating is submissive, vague, and rarely letting other people know what the person really thinks, feels, or wants, because of the belief that if people really cared they would know what he or she wanted, and magically provide it. There is an abdication of responsibility for getting one's own needs met, and when they remain unmet, the passive position is to harbor resentment. There is also a tendency to assume a martyr-like attitude, particularly after having invited people to walk all over him or her. The unwillingness to state his or her position clearly comes from the person's low self-esteem and lack of self-confidence.

The *passive-aggressive* style of relating is geared to inducing guilt feelings in other people. There is a manipulative quality inasmuch as the person implies that the other person is inconsiderate, unkind and uncaring, and has a duty to cater to the passive-aggressive individual's needs. The manipulative behavior has developed out of a habitual way of attempting to get needs met, which is again based on low self-esteem and inability to communicate with others in a more straightforward way, often because of holding back feelings of anger which have no acceptable channel of expression, due to excessive unresolved conflict.

Learning to be more assertive seemed to be of the most obvious value to many clients I have seen in London. Having the confidence to recognize one's own right as well as need to be treated respectfully by others helped some clients behave differently in their relationships. Clients learned rapidly that they could not necessarily change other people in their lives, but they could *risk* responding differently to familiar situations and perhaps limit the extent to which others could put them down.

In my work with clients with multiple sclerosis and their partners, much time has been spent in therapy sessions letting them know that it may be wasted effort to feel angry and resentful about their partners' lack of recognition of their needs, if they have not actually communicated to them what those needs are. Many people feel foolish spelling out their needs. Nevertheless, they expect people to fulfil them 'instinctively'.

Once my clients grasped that they were using unrealistic rules in relationships and accepted the responsibility of telling people in their lives what they needed, they gradually began to feel better about themselves and less resentful towards others. For example, many were surprised to see how willing their partners were to comply, once they were clear as to what it was that was wanted. It could have been more help with the housework, more time for one self, more or less physical intimacy, or a request for an occasional cup of coffee to be made for the spouse by the partner with a physical disability, if that was possible.

It was the kind of changes I have described that often resulted in clients feeling better about themselves and others. There was less resentment, and subsequently less guilt about the resentment. A shift took place, so that clients began changing themselves rather than passively waiting for others to change, or a miracle to take place.

What is also very important in my work, is helping people understand that they do have the right to say, "No," and that others also have the right to tell them, "No." There is a fairly widespread belief that people will feel hurt if their request is denied. To prevent the other person's hurt, the belief goes, it will be better to delay saying, "No," until the very last minute, or to simply avoid him or her in the hope that the avoidance will serve as an effective hint. Remember, this is supposed to be the kinder option.

I wish it were needless to say that it is inconsiderate and irrational to delay letting another person know that a request has been denied, because it reduces the time he or she has to get it met elsewhere. People seem to believe they will be punished if they say, "No," and very often that goes back to some earlier ways parental and authoritative figures had of disciplining them when they were children. Many people have to be taught that those days are over and they are now adults and can work out their own new, fair rules for themselves. I advocate the value of openness, honesty and respectful directness, rather than second-guessing, mind-reading and devious behaviors.

Summary

In this chapter a number of emotional issues were described. The uniqueness of each individual was demonstrated, leaving counselors at times feeling in awe of their clients. Since we can only know a fraction of another's experience at any given moment in time, I advocated *not knowing* as potentially the most helpful stance for counselors.

A sample of psychological concepts was selected to provide some background to appreciating the importance of theories of personalities when working psychotherapeutically with clients. Anxiety was discussed using Rogers' example of a mother who developed psychosomatic symptoms when her self-concept did not correspond with her experience or feelings. It was shown how anxiety developed out of incongruence.

Conditions of worth was another term used by Rogers. Concepts he developed were presented in the hope that more and more counselors would continue to recognize the importance of adhering to models of the mind that can help clients understand and reduce their distress. Depression was considered as a valid emotion that is triggered off by loss, and the contribution of assertiveness to personal growth was emphasized. Careful distinctions were made between aggressive, passive, and passive-aggressive styles of relating, so that the valued position of being true to one self was shown to be central to being assertive, as well as to person-centered personal growth work.

CHAPTER
SEVEN

Communicating Verbally and Nonverbally with Clients

In order to practise counseling and psychotherapy, there are certain essential skills that must be acquired. The pertinent verbal and nonverbal communication skills are described in detail, followed by a section focusing on the complexities of staying with feelings at an affective level, rather than shifting into feelings talk at a cognitive level.

Communicating Verbally

In my view, the willingness to continuously develop one's verbal skills is a requirement for all counselors and psychotherapists. What we offer clients, along with our attitudes are our words. Out of these words, the burden falls on them to make sense of what we have communicated. Therefore, it is our responsibility to assure that we have expressed what we wanted to say as clearly and concisely as possible.

Speaking clearly and concisely is a skill that comes from close and ongoing attention to what people say, and what we want to say. It means thinking before we speak. It has to do with an awareness of the power of the unconscious and recognizing that what we often want to say has more to do with our own processes than the client's. Therefore, we need to give ourselves time, before the words have impulsively escaped us.

All too often, counselors and psychotherapists respond to client's in a confusing and jumbled way, leaving clients feeling confused and with decreased self-esteem. Even worse, clients are accused of being confused and mixed-up when it was in fact the therapist who had not concentrated well enough on material which was understandable. That material is then communicated back to the client in a confused and mixed-up way leading to an unsatisfactory working relationship.

For many people the painstaking effort of taking the time to carefully consider the meanings of our words before we speak will perhaps sound horribly contrived. It could be said that we may then be compromising spontaneity, genuineness, and congruence. Others advocate reliance on their intuition. Those who dwell on their intuitiveness in responding to clients alarm me, since intuition has more to do with the counselor's psychological process than the client's. In fact, I would go further and suggest that most unsatisfactory psychotherapeutic relationships faltered because of the therapist's heavily weighted reliance on intuition as compared with a solid theoretical base and careful attention to the client in his or her own right.

My experience has been different. Over the years I chose not to speak until I had sufficiently formulated interventions that appeared to be of sufficient use to clients to communicate to them that I was in the process of understanding their communications, and endeavoring to facilitate their process, rather than take it over. The spontaneity, genuineness, and congruence were communicated gradually, inasmuch as it was true that I was allowing myself to be sufficiently open to my own awareness so that I could consider the implications and accuracy of my words for them before imparting them.

The fact is that communicating clearly using everyday language improves with practice. Over time it is possible to go through these painstaking efforts without them feeling so awesome. That does not mean to say I always succeed in terms of being accurate and clear. What has helped me maintain these skills has been the self-discipline I imposed in terms of writing *verbatim* accounts of therapy sessions. In order to reproduce a session after the client leaves, the therapist will have very carefully attended to what the client was communicating. The most painful, and at the same time most valuable part, was writing down what the therapist said. By writing down so many unclear, unhelpful interventions I had made in sessions, it quickly reduced them in subsequent sessions, since it enabled me to understand how my own frame of reference was interfering with the client's processing.

For me, it was being very strict with myself that initially resulted in fewer interventions. I needed time and experience to practise intervening in ways that would be closest to appreciating clients' experiences. It was reproducing sessions in writing as accurately as I could that facilitated the learning experience for me more than anything else. I recognized the importance of learning to understand the way each client expressed himself or herself, and the importance of attending to how each client used words and nonverbal communications to self-explore. In other words,

I practised maintaining an empathic stance not only when I was with clients, but I remained empathic in writing up each session so as to understand its significance from each client's frame of reference rather than my own.

I must emphasize that I cannot imagine that a time will arrive while I continue to work as a psychotherapist when I will be able to relax in the sense of automatically being psychotherapeutic. That is what makes the work challenging, rewarding and stimulating. No matter how experienced the counselor or psychotherapist, we cannot anticipate what a session will be like, whether it is the first, or the one-hundred and first, with a particular client. Each session requires a very special kind of concentration and consideration with due regard for the client's process.

Communicating Nonverbally

Silence is important. It is perhaps the most valuable and rare resource counselors have to offer. There are very few places where people can go and be guaranteed of getting most of the talking time; very few, indeed. The following scenario is probably all too familiar, where preparation is made to see a professional or authority figure from either the health professions or any other private or public service, for example, a lawyer, accountant, or social security official.

People go to considerable trouble to make the necessary arrangements to seek out advice and help. Very often, the first hurdle upon arrival is having to wait and experience the anxiety of wondering whether or not they are expected. The next part of the process is being invited to the person in authority's desk or office, in either a public or private place, where the person must state or restate the reason for the visit. After only a minute or two, the person in authority is likely to interrupt and give all kinds of advice and suggestions, based on minimal information. As he or she listens, other related questions and issues probably come to mind. Depending on the personality of the individual concerned, particularly with regard to level of self-confidence, self-esteem, assertiveness and verbal skills, he or she may or may not be able to interrupt the authority figure to clarify the issue and ask more specific questions.

Unfortunately, no matter how assertive the individual who seeks out professional help, there is no guarantee that he or she will get another word in edgewise. The more important the meeting or consultation, the more likely that strong emotions will be stirred up by what is being communicated by the authority figure. If, for example, it has to do with one's health, property, housing, or benefits, the emotional reactions are likely to be quite intense and may render him or her speechless, unable to voice any more questions, let alone interrupt the clever person providing the lecture about these very personal and sensitive issues.

Professionals and authority figures all too often drift off into jargon only they and their colleagues seem to understand and leave clients feeling too ignorant to ask what may sound like trivial questions, but are nevertheless very important concerns. In a twenty-minute consultation, it is not unusual for the client to get only five minutes of the talking time. The rest of the time, he or she is expected to listen submissively to the wise words of the person who has been consulted. Remember, these are the people we go to when we have important issues 'to talk through.'

I still find myself in this position from time to time when dealing with personal issues of emotional significance. I have developed strategies to reduce the likelihood of being overwhelmed by other people's expertise at times of need, but they are not foolproof. In the end, the only safeguard rests with the professional, and his or her willingness to listen to what clients need to communicate to them, and to facilitate communication rather than distort it by rushing us so that the full picture fails to emerge.

The idea of being silent makes some counselors and psychotherapists feel uncomfortable. Many health and mental health professionals I have taught began by expressing dissatisfaction at not knowing what they should be saying to distressed patients. The idea of being silent did not appear helpful to them, because of feeling both foolish and lazy. My task is to help them use silence for the good of their patients and to enable them to feel differently about not talking most of the time to or for patients. How can anyone feel foolish and lazy in a working silence? We are silent because we are concentrating and attending to what is being communicated to us in order to better understand and facilitate patients' emotional processes.

In my own work, I welcome pauses and silences as valuable times in the session when I can replay, in my own mind, all that has transpired between the client and me since his or her arrival for the psychotherapy session. It is during those silences when I am most likely to get back in touch with any problematic interventions I may have made that the client may be working through either consciously or unconsciously. Silences give me time to formulate interventions that may facilitate the client's process, and silences also give the client time to reflect and then comment on the process.

Along with silence, in order to create a working space, another useful nonverbal communication has to do with the counselor or therapist frequently averting his or her eyes, instead of maintaining continuous eye contact with the client throughout sessions. It is only if the counselor can back off enough that the possibility will arise for clients to get more in touch with themselves.

Each client requires a different amount of eye contact while getting started. Too much can inadvertently invite clients into less therapeutic and more social relationships. A productive counseling or therapy session is not defined by how comfortable or uncomfortable it was for one or both participants, but more importantly, by whether or not clients were provided with the kind of space and atmosphere that increased the likelihood of them discovering something of themselves for themselves.

There is a great deal of concern about the misuse of silence and limited eye contact. People have rightly complained about these nonverbal communications being used in punitive, controlling and hostile ways. All I can say about that is if, after a few sessions, clients feel a good deal of hostility coming from the counselor, which is not balanced by any facilitating behaviors, then perhaps they are not in a good working relationship. The likelihood is that the counselor is hostile, controlling and punitive. However, clients need to search within themselves to see if the hostility, punishing and controlling characteristics are not coming from themselves and being projected onto the counselor before making too hasty a retreat. Even if clients believe these traits they see in the therapist might be projections, they still have to see whether or not the counselor seems up to helping them understand more about themselves.

When silence and limited eye contact are provided with the wish to be of help, clients usually sense it within the first few sessions. If they wish to self-explore, they soon learn how to make the best use of these rare resources - the presence of another human being who can be with them empathically allowing them to discover themselves *at their own pace*. Interestingly enough, it is within this climate that counselors and therapists create a calm climate enabling clients to discover meaningful parts of themselves and to focus on them long enough to begin to understand, as well as experience whatever intense feelings are present.

The calm serves as a kind of natural anesthetic allowing clients to tolerate moving through sensitive areas, in order to discover more and more about themselves. It is like going to the dentist in order to correct a dental problem. We know it will be uncomfortable and may hurt. We do it because once the cause of the pain, the infection, is treated, it is less likely that it will get worse. Similarly with emotional pain. If we avoid it and deny it for too long, it may get worse. Psychotherapy clients are sensible enough to take notice of symptoms, rather than ignore them, and work towards their integration so as to prevent the likelihood of their reappearance in such an unfriendly, incomprehensible way again.

Whoever said that people who go into counseling and psychotherapy are self-indulgent? It takes a lot of courage to take a good look at one self with a view to change. There's nothing self-indulgent about that. One might just as well say that it is self-indulgent to get regular health check-ups.

Communicating Feelings

Feelings are nonverbal. Yet, clients are expected to come along and put into words how they feel. Words can only be an approximation, which is why it is so important to stay with the words they use, rather than introducing new ones. In order to describe their feelings, clients must translate them into words. It can be seen, therefore, how easy it would be for either a directive, or an overzealous nondirective, counselor to introduce new words. The client may accept the counselor's words which could actually be further removed from the original meaning than the client's. Gradually, there is an increasing probability that the client will use the counselor's language and begin to experience the counselor's feelings rather than his or her own.

For example, the client may say that he or she feels *sad* about a recent event. The counselor may respond by saying that the client sounds *depressed.* The client may then comply with the counselor's need to speak about depression, and neither of them may remember that what the client was actually experiencing was a feeling approximating sadness. On my counseling courses I try to expand participants' vocabularies for words expressing emotion. Much of the time, people hardly pay attention to the sorts of words they use and the different parts of the mind which their words represent. Counselors and psychotherapists need to attend to language in particular ways, in order to better understand clients' communications, as well as their own, in the psychotherapy relationship.

Nelson-Jones (1983) included a very useful exercise to explore "feelings talk" vocabulary which stressed how errors in understanding the intensity of a feeling can be as unhelpful as misunderstanding the sort of emotion the client is experiencing. In his example, he demonstrated how unhelpful it would be to let someone know you recognize how nervous they feel when they are actually 'panic-stricken'.

Often newly qualified counselors and psychotherapists only recognize certain words and phrases as direct representations of emotions. Some of the most obvious ones include the following feelings: resentful, sad, afraid, frightened, worried, paranoid, lonely, angry, distressed, unhappy, guilty, desperate, frustrated, isolated, panic-stricken, stressed and tense. Less obvious feeling words and phrases include: upset, troubled, uneasy, pleased, satiated, disappointed, unsure, at odds with myself, helpless, unappreciated, undesirable, hopeless, difficult, hurt, envious, curious, mixed, apprehensive, different, maternal, paternal, important, unimportant, jealous, involved, uninvolved, loveable, unlovable, trapped, surprised, misunderstood, respected, and vulnerable.

Looking at these feeling words and phrases, it may be hard to believe that any of them would not immediately be recognized as direct representations of emotional life. However, in my courses I repeatedly see how easy it is for participants practising their counseling skills to miss them, because the words and phrases get thrown in with a mass of material. The counselor's or therapist's ability to pick up the subtle feelings clients try to communicate depends mostly on his or her listening skills.

An inexperienced counselor or therapist may misinterpret my meaning here and consider the possibility that clients deliberately attempt to mislead us, by rapidly expressing their feelings amid a mass of material. Clients usually do not hear themselves. They also are oblivious to whether or not they are using feeling words, because it is hoped that they are simply speaking as freely as they can. Our job is to listen in a way that increases the likelihood of receiving the message. That is why I consider it important to string feeling words together on these pages. The more aware we are that almost any word can be used to represent an emotion, the more intent we will be on listening to our clients, rather than wanting to give them our words and feelings.

In considering clients who do not say very much, the main feeling to stay with is the dislike of having to talk, and being silent some of the time may also be experienced as empathic. There are also clients who start out using very few feeling words, but prefer to offer a report of what has happened in their lives that is devoid of feeling or emotion. The therapist's task then is somewhat different. It becomes necessary to pick up nonverbal cues to try to empathize with the client on a feeling level. Tone of voice, gestures and facial expression may communicate how the client feels about what he or she is reporting. Given a serious tone of voice, a lack of gestures, and a concerned look on the client's face, I may take the risk of saying that it sounds like what he or she has been telling me is very important to him or her. If that is so, I have then successfully linked up with the client's emotions, and have enabled him or her to get just beneath the surface increasing the likelihood that the client will continue to communicate with me at an emotional rather than a cognitive level.

There are clients who articulate clearly when communicating feelings; then the skill of the counselor has to do with staying close to their language in terms of the words they use to express emotions. With clients who excel in the use of language, there may be a tendency for the counselor to want to compete linguistically and to perhaps enjoy the exchange of words. Our discipline requires us to stay with our clients' emotional lives and not to be distracted by any special talents they have. In other words, although it might have been supposed that communicating in psychotherapy with articulate clients would move the process along, difficulties in achieving some level of accuracy in understanding their meanings still prevail, and just as much attention and concentration is needed.

There are clients who use some feeling words, but in a conservative sort of way, and an example follows:

CLIENT: *(Looking out of the window, looking tired, sighs). Sometimes I think it would be better not to think about how I feel. I have a very demanding job and I do enjoy it. No, that's the wrong word. (Sounds annoyed) I wouldn't say I'm enjoying it at the moment. There's too much paperwork. That means I can never feel satisfied at the end of the day, because there's always administrative work left over. But I do like working in the hospital and treating patients. (Sounds embarrassed and shifts in the chair) It would be fine if other things in my life weren't so pressurized. My parents-in-law are quite a worry right now. I think I've told you that they are getting more and more frail. (Looks exasperated) I try to keep an eye on them as much as I can, but then I'm left feeling guilty because I'm not spending enough time with my parents who are also not as young as they used to be. It's all a bit much sometimes. (Throws her hands up in the air just for an instant) I wish I could lie down and sleep for a week. If only someone else could step in and do something for a change.*

(Shrugs her shoulders) I don't really mean that. It's just that sometimes it feels like it's all too much for me. (Compassionately) I love my parents very much and I'm fond of my parents-in-law too. I hate to watch them grow old. Sometimes I wish I could do more for them.

THERAPIST: *You've been talking about the various demands that are presently being made of you. There's your work, which although can be very satisfying, lately has been less so because, I think, of some administrative overload you mentioned. And there's the older generation in your family - your parents, and your parents-in-*

law, and your feelings of responsibility and love for them. Mostly while I've been listening to you, today, I've heard how very tired you are right now, and you said, you put it this way, that if only someone could take over, so you could sleep for a week.

CLIENT: *Oh, yes! That would be so nice right now. I truly am exhausted. There's another, well, not problem - but . . . Oh, this is hard to know how to explain. (**Silence**) It's just that sometimes I feel resentful because there are other people in the family who could be taking on some of the responsibility and are not. I hate to sound petty, but . . . (**Laughs**) Oh, here I go, feeling sorry for myself.*

THERAPIST: *It really is hard for you to talk about feeling resentful. You said you feel like you're being petty. I certainly recognize your discomfort in talking about other family members who you said are not taking on some of the responsibility and perhaps easing some of the pressure off you.*

CLIENT: *I don't like talking about other people. I come here to talk about myself and when I find myself bringing in others, I start to feel disloyal.*

Numerous feelings were communicated in the above example.

The therapist had to estimate the level at which to respond to the client. Some of the feelings she had communicated included guilt, feeling worn out, mixed feelings, exasperation, she felt used, compassion, upset, sad, frightened, not knowing what to do, apprehensive as to how things would turn out, embarrassed at exposing herself to the counselor, feeling judged, afraid of being criticized, self-critical, wanting someone to take care of her, and angry. It was the counselor's job to be aware of these feelings and to make a decision as to which appeared to be the strongest and most conscious at the moment, so as to be able to let the client know she had been heard. The counselor needed to be sensitive to the client's capacity for self-blame and in building a therapeutic relationship, to initially stay with her feelings of exasperation, uncertainty, and apprehension.

The client reported feeling worn out by the responsibilities she had taken on to keep an eye on her elderly parents-in-law, while at the same time her own parents required considerable attention, and she held a demanding full-time job. Her tone of voice suggested that she felt she had no right to complain and sounded somewhat guilty even admitting that she was worn out. Her facial expressions were mixed. She looked at times exasperated in terms of the demands being made upon her which she herself had to some extent invited, and there was an expression of compassion for the elderly relatives needing care. Her gestures were consistent with her tone of voice and facial expressions. She shrugged her shoulders, shifted in her chair, and very quickly and lightly threw her hands up in the air, so quickly that the movement could have gone unnoticed.

I would most certainly begin with empathizing with how worn out the client felt since that also represented how she felt physically at the time and was the easiest and most benign feeling for her to hear back. By benign, I mean that she was unlikely to feel criticized upon experiencing the counselor as sensitive to how worn out she felt. At the same time, by communicating at that level, the client may also have experienced the counselor as sensitive to her wish to be taken care of, and the possibility presented itself that the counselor might be a compassionate person with the capacity to understand without making harsh judgments, and someone who truly wanted to be of help.

Once the client sensed that the counselor had heard all that she had said, she was likely to continue, and again the counselor's task was to attend to the dominant feelings that she expressed next. She might have spoken more about feeling worn out and how that was impacting on her life. On the other hand, since that seemed to be well understood by the counselor she may have moved on to explore some other feelings.

In my view, the least helpful initial intervention would have been to threaten the client by saying back to her that she sounded angry about all the responsibilities she had. That is only acceptable when clients are very much aware of those feelings, but in the example above, the client seemed less aware of her anger in her opening remarks. Had the counselor commented on it too soon, she may well have believed that the counselor was judging her, because she possibly would not have recalled having communicated feelings of anger to the counselor, since it was communicated nonverbally and was outside her awareness.

The main problem with saying back what was least conscious was that it was too soon to assume that the client felt that way. Thus far, she had merely indicated that the strong negative feelings could be present. I advocate a tentative approach that is facilitative, rather than a threatening one that fails to recognize the client's vulnerability.

It is important to remember that defences are unconscious mechanisms that get put into effect, reflexively, when we feel dangers threatening us either from within ourselves or from the external world. Usually, the danger comes in part from within and without. For example, when anticipating failure, an individual may defend against powerful feelings of inadequacy that come from within by avoiding the examination or interview. When experiencing loss, in terms of the death of a loved one, we may defend against the inner pain by denying the reality of the loss and delaying the realization of it until such time as some inner adaptation has taken place to make it possible for us to tolerate the pain. Defensive behavior can be adaptive and maladaptive. In the way I work, I prefer to assume that if a client is in a defensive mode, the reaction is probably adaptive since how much pain can be tolerated is best automatically monitored by the client by defence mechanisms that are readily available.

It does not take any clinical skill to notice when somebody is being defensive. Defensive behavior is usually obvious to everyone excepting the person exhibiting it. Therefore it is not helpful to say to someone who is being defensive, "You're being defensive," because that will make the person more defensive and what is more, the individual will not be impressed by your observation. This is such an important issue, an example follows highlighting the importance of being sensitive to clients' defences and not confronting them with the underlying hurt before they are ready to become aware of it for themselves:

CLIENT: *(Mr. Steele has been attending weekly counseling sessions over the past four months. His wife was terminally ill and had been told she had six more months to live. Mr. S. had been using the sessions to help him prepare for the eventuality of his wife's death) (Telephones counselor) Hello. This is Frank Steele. I'm calling to let you know that . . . my wife . . . she . . . em . . . she died this morning.*

COUNSELOR: *Oh, I'm really sorry to hear that. (Pause)*

CLIENT: *I wanted to let you know. (Pause) I'll be there Tuesday for my session, but I wanted to . . . (Pause)*

COUNSELOR: *I can hear how difficult this is for you. I'll see you Tuesday.*

CLIENT: *Bye.*

COUNSELOR: *Bye.*

CLIENT: *(Enters counselor's office on Tuesday) (Looks unwell, untidy, unshaven and a bit shaky on his feet). (Speaking loudly) Well, I phoned you and I told you that my wife died. And I want you to know that these sessions have really helped. I'm handling it just great. I'm okay. I really am okay.*

COUNSELOR: *(Recognizes that Mr. S is probably still in shock and probably unaware of how loudly he is speaking and how distraught he looks) (Pause) That's right. You called me and told me she had died and I said how sorry I was.*

CLIENT: *Yes, but you know what. I'm handling it so well. I've made the funeral plans. It's going to be some funeral. I've informed most of our friends and relatives and everything's under control. Everything.*

COUNSELOR: *It sounds like you're relieved at the way you're handling it. You said these sessions really helped. You've made the funeral plans, informed people, and you want me to know that you're handling your wife's death really well.*

CLIENT: *That's right. I'm fine. I'm just fine. (Silence) (Talks in great detail about the last days and hours of his wife's life and her death). (Twenty minutes have passed with the counselor listening; no need to intervene.) (Client places his hands over his face and leans forward). (Speaks quietly) You know, when I came in here today I told you I feel fine. I feel terrible. Oh so terrible. What am I going to do? (Cries) I already miss her so much. (Sobbing quietly)*

COUNSELOR: *You've talked about the last days you and your wife had together and in going through all of the important moments you have got more in touch with your sorrow and with your pain.*

CLIENT: *I never knew it could hurt this much.*

The example demonstrates the importance of respecting the client's defences so that he can work at his own pace. Had the counselor confronted the client at the outset by saying that although the client was saying that he was handling it okay, both of them really knew he was feeling distraught, the client may have become angry and would have then been unable to get in touch with his feelings during the session.

Often when clients' defences are not respected, sessions turn into struggles between counselors and clients, while the former insist on telling clients what they really feel. In that way, counselors become engaged in an intellectual conversation with clients about clients' feelings which has nothing to do with facilitating anyone's emotional process. In order to get more deeply in touch with one's emotional life, communications need to be appreciated as meaningful and valid, be they verbal or nonverbal, defensive or unguarded.

In working psychotherapeutically, I have found it helpful for clients when I have reflected feelings back using words that are unlikely to be heard as critical, unless they are using those words themselves. Therefore, if clients sound resentful, angry, or jealous, I am unlikely to reflect back those feelings using those words. Instead, I will respond by saying that they seem to be experiencing some difficult feelings that seem to be making them feel uncomfortable. Often, the use of neutral words, referred to earlier as less obvious feeling words, succeed in keeping clients in touch with their feelings without them feeling too threatened by them. As with the example of the man whose wife had died, often after twenty or forty minutes, when clients are left to work at their own pace, they may discover for themselves feelings of anger, resentment, or jealousy and comment upon them.

On Bereavement

Nothing is so painful as watching those close to us grieve. We feel so helpless, so sad, so unhappy for them. I will try to put a whole range of feelings into words. With words people can tell their loved ones what they feel, and then they can risk talking about their reactions to the death of someone special. It makes sense that people find themselves unable to talk to the mourner. Words sound so trivial compared to the powerful waves of feelings swelling up inside.

Dying is something which affects us throughout life. It is an important part of living, understanding our reactions to dying. The bereaved will respond to each death differently. Each loss will hold different meanings for us. Our feelings will vary. That is why it is so difficult when more than one loved one has died at any given time. For example, more than one member of your family may have died in a fire in the home, and you may have survived. The problems in mourning for more than one person at a time are great because your relationship with each member of the family was different, because each person and each relationship are unique.

No one can tell those who are bereaved how they should feel, nor would it be helpful to deny the fact that most of us have mixed emotions. Often, when grief is spoken about, it is incorrectly assumed that the relationship between the person who died and the partner, child, parent or friend, was a good and happy one.

The fact is that unsatisfactory relationships are familiar to all of us. Therefore, those who grieve for loved ones with whom the relationship was unsatisfactory may feel at a loss as to how to respond or react to the loss. The grief process then is indeed difficult. At such times, the bereaved need people who can help them express their mixed and confused feelings. Otherwise, they are left feeling isolated and less entitled to the comfort and support of those around them.

People die at different stages of life - old age, middle age, young adulthood, the teenage years, childhood, infancy, the newborn and the not yet born. People of all ages grieve for partners, parents, siblings, children, infants, babies, the stillborn, miscarriages, and aborted pregnancies.

The causes of death vary tremendously. Our reactions to each death are affected by how the person died. Was it an illness, an accident; sudden or prolonged; murder or suicide? The way we die affects the way we mourn and grieve.

Yes, it is painful but stay with the pain. Learn more about it. If it is pushed back and we pretend it does not hurt it will only get worse. One then begins to feel a loss of one's own self. So hang on. Feelings are important. Respect them. Out of pain comes growth. Together, in these pages, all of us can begin to work through our grief for none of us has been untouched by loss.

Grief is expressed differently by each individual. Nevertheless, researchers have identified some of the most frequently experienced reactions to death. The initial reaction is shock. Shock can be experienced as if it were actual physical pain. People have reported having felt 'torn apart'.

Shock can be expressed in a variety of ways. One person may become distant; another may respond angrily and express rage; yet others may appear to remain calm and accepting, and behave in a controlled, cooperative manner. All of these expressions of grief are valid. Let's not evaluate who seems to be handling it best. There is no 'best' way.

Each of us seems to initially respond to our deepest sadnesses in a reflexive way. It would be unfair to commend one type of response and condemn another. While in shock, the person's body and mind are automatically finding ways of adapting to the meaning of the loss thus enabling the person to go through the grief process with the goal of coping.

There is no set time that shock lasts. That phase of grieving does not go on in isolation. Thus, it is not at all obvious whether or not it has subsided.

To be supportive to someone in shock, it is important not to over-react. It is better to stay with the person in a calm, non-demanding manner, perhaps silently communicating acceptance of the understandable overwhelming flood of emotions which may have temporarily stopped the person in his or her tracks, leaving a sense of numbness and a state of disbelief.

Although the person may have understood the fact of the loved one's death, people close are sometimes perplexed when the bereaved nevertheless seems to act as if the loved one is alive. The newly bereaved cannot take in what has happened at an emotional level as quickly as he or she can intellectually grasp the fact. This phenomenon can be seen on a daily basis in the way we handle minor disappointments.

An example of the above might be a situation where a friend cancels an outing to a special place of interest at short notice. Intellectually you may respond by grasping the fact and then you might comfort yourself by either telling yourself that it really wasn't that important anyway, or you might begin plans for some future date. Some hours or days later you may be surprised to find yourself still behaving *as if* you were going on the outing. You may have a fleeting thought reminding you to gather the appropriate clothes, for example. As you recall the fact that it's been cancelled, you may feel embarrassed, frightened, or confused by your 'forgetfulness'.

The easiest way to understand the above example has to do with the tendency to behave in ways that are familiar rather than adopting new behaviors and reactions to each life event. If someone has been used to living at home with parents, brothers and sisters, and pets for the last fifteen years and a sister dies, it will take time emotionally to accept and to develop behaviors and reactions that do not automatically include her *as if* she were still alive.

As the reality of the situation strengthens, a mixture of feelings is experienced by the newly bereaved. Anger and feelings of helplessness are most likely. Unfortunately, the bereaved is now faced with an additional problem or conflict, one which may be outside of his or her awareness, but nevertheless a very important issue.

The expression of feelings is not readily tolerated, and tends to be avoided, possibly because feelings are so difficult to understand. The task of grieving becomes even more problematic if the bereaved feels it necessary to inhibit either a strong need to cry or shout or scream. Surely this is not a time to demonstrate 'good manners', whatever that means. It is important to feel free to cry out or express anger at a time when one is in so much pain. If these feelings are present, but not expressed, they build up and sometimes are converted into more unpleasant reactions such as sleeplessness, inability to eat, or headaches, to name a few. It seems unfair to discourage people from expressing painful feelings for the sake of those around them.

The expression of anger often seems to conjure up all kinds of violent images. Ordinarily, anger is expressed in the following way: a person looks angry, because of the facial expression and body posture. The words expressed are angry inasmuch as direct, accusatory, and may contain expletives. For example, an angry response made by someone recently bereaved may take the following form:

*It's not fair. They didn't do enough. Nobody cared enough. Why did they let him die? I hate them. I wish **they** were dead, not him! The hell with them. I'll **never** forgive them.*

This angry outburst hurts no one, but it does afford the newly bereaved some release of pent-up emotions. Blaming may be a first step to eventually accepting that a loved one's death was or was not due to negligence or lack of care. People *need* to express their profound disappointment with words, tears, or both. It is a more honest approach and allows for a healthier outcome.

There are, of course, those who will only cry or acknowledge anger in private. They should not be coerced into a more public display. The point is that those who can express themselves in the company of supportive individuals should not be stopped. Showing one's emotions to trusted friends and relatives is an important first step to healing.

Many people are instructed by those close to them not to cry nor to feel angry. Subsequently, clinical psychologists and other psychotherapists and counselors, see more and more people who were not permitted by their spouses, or parents, or both, to express themselves emotionally. Thus they became labelled 'depressed', 'anxious' (or worse) by those closest to them. It is not surprising then that unwanted symptoms tend to develop, most particularly low self-esteem.

Along with the emotional reactions to the death of someone close, the newly bereaved experience some quite frightening physical sensations. This is a time of inner turmoil. It is not unusual to experience tightness in the chest, oversensitivity to noise, lack of energy, breathlessness, loss of appetite, and sleep disturbance. Some newly bereaved experience physical complaints which the deceased experienced.

All of the above is accompanied by feelings of guilt and anxiety. Interspersed with angry feelings toward others, the newly bereaved now has thoughts which begin, *"If only I had . . . "*, or, *"What if I had . . . ?"*, or, *"It's my fault . . . "*. Newly bereaved are also called *'survivors'*. Those who survive tend to experience some guilt about those who did not. As indicated earlier, all of the reactions mentioned so far, and many more, seem to be going on simultaneously resulting in an overall feeling of confusion. The strong sense of the presence of the deceased adds to the newly bereaved's disorganized state. Many people report seeing the deceased and these hallucinations are considered a normal and sometimes helpful part of the process.

It is important to let the newly bereaved know that these reactions do not mean that he or she is going crazy. At the same time it is important not to minimize how frightened and vulnerable the person is. This needs to be done without patronizing or pitying the person. It is hard to get it right all of the time when supporting someone in distress, but if we get it right some of the time it will become more likely that the grief process will be facilitated.

How can anyone know whether or not he or she is being truly helpful to the newly bereaved? The same question can be asked of any psychotherapist or counselor in their work. Facilitating another person's emotional growth is the work of a therapist and also it is the work of the friend or relative of the newly bereaved.

Facilitating another person's emotional growth means being with someone who is in some kind of process - for example, the grief process, and encouraging him or her to describe the experience and accompanying feelings. As the person speaks about the emotional and physical painful reactions to the loss, it becomes possible to reflect on the meanings of the loss and to gradually move from a state of disorganization to reorganization.

The journey through the confusion and disorientation will often be a difficult one, but nevertheless necessary for satisfactory reorganization. Therefore, at the time when we may actually be of most help is the very time when the newly bereaved will appear to be the least grateful to us for standing by. To be most effective, our own needs for gratitude need to be put aside. The newly bereaved is too stretched to have the burden of also having to reassure and thank us. It might happen, but let us not think any the worse of the person if he or she does not. In fact, let's take it as a compliment that we are facilitating the grief process well enough so that good manners have temporarily lapsed in order to concentrate efforts entirely on the healing, or the grief process.

Gradually, the newly bereaved, with the support of relatives, friends, and the community, begins to cope with life without the deceased. Once the person begins to reconnect with the environment and is allowed to give up the role of 'mourner', the last stage of grieving has been reached. Do not despair if there is a sudden relapse and the person slips back to an earlier stage of grieving. Sliding backwards and forwards is natural in emotional development.

Setbacks cannot be avoided. There are so many triggers in daily life that can potentially rekindle the pain of grief. The sight of places and people will suddenly bring back memories of the deceased reminding the bereaved how much he or she is missed.

Support for the bereaved should not be withdrawn as soon as coping behavior is seen. Some people experience grief most painfully either weeks, months, or years after the bereavement, especially around the times of anniversaries and birthdays.

People never actually get over the death of loved ones. There is always a gap felt inside that stands for the person. We do, however, survive. It hurts less with time, but is not forgotten. Why would anyone want to forget the feelings and memories associated with those they loved?

Dying is a part of living. As we survive the deaths of some of those close and dear to us, we begin to accept our own mortality and so prepare for the fact that we, too, one day will die.

The death of a partner who lived with the bereaved is usually going to have far more consequences than the death of a friend or relative outside of the home. This statement is based on the observation that people who live together, whether married or cohabiting, tend to divide the tasks of living between them. The resources of both individuals are used. Often, one attends to tasks which are more interesting to that partner, while the other tends to tasks which are of more interest to him or her.

For example, one person usually looks after the payment of house bills and the partner might look after the maintenance of the car and garden. It is likely that when a partner dies, the other has to learn skills which he or she has not yet needed to put to use, because that was the partner's job. The loss of a partner often includes loss of income. Subsequently, the death of a partner means a change in the survivor's lifestyle. Also, a loss of a partner is often accompanied by a loss of identity and role, and, at least temporarily, loss of self-esteem.

The survivor gradually comes to view himself or herself as a separate person. In any partnership, people's separateness is not so clear. It is hard getting used to saying, 'me' most of the time when partners have been used to talking about 'us'.

Thus it can be seen that a bereavement can result in a multitude of simultaneous reactions. Emotional reactions to the loss of the loved person have been discussed. When practical issues are added on, however, a fuller picture of the implications of the loss emerges.

There are, of course, instances where the death of a partner can bring about relief to the survivor. Many people find themselves stuck in relationships where they are physically and emotionally abused. It takes considerable strength and planning to leave such a relationship. Partners are often afraid to leave. When a feared and violent partner dies, the survivor will nevertheless experience grief, but the feelings of yearning and despair may be significantly reduced.

Many families today are not made up of two adult partners. One-parent families abound. The parent's main support may come from someone outside of the home in these circumstances. The single parent might have already experienced the bereavement of the partner who died or left. Perhaps the single parent's mother or father became the main supportive figure after the loss. If so, the death of the parent would be almost as devastating as the initial loss. Practical as well as emotional support would have gone.

During our lives people we love and care about die, many of whom are not directly involved in our day-to-day lives. A friend, grandparent, cousin, uncle, niece, colleague, neighbor, or even a public figure not known to us personally, may die causing us untold grief. In these instances, our reactions are primarily emotional. What seems to happen is an instantaneous identification with the immediate survivor whereby there occurs a temporary experience of the pain of the loss as if it were our own. Such suffering is intense. The death of someone we know brings to mind all the feelings that have been experienced with previous losses. Also, it presses us to face the eventuality of our own death.

When a child dies a family is thrown into the depths of despair. There is a sense of order in life - one generation follows another. When this pattern dramatically changes, the pain felt by the survivors is unspeakable. In today's society we react to the death of a child as most unnatural. Not so long ago, it was considered quite natural that only some children would enter adulthood.

In both two-parent and one-parent homes, the focus tends to be on the children. The goal of living seems to revolve around the children's development, passing on from one school year to the next, learning how to cope in society, and planning on the kinds of work they will do so as to eventually look after themselves and become independent.

Up until the age of six, children tend to be dependent upon the parent or caretaker for all of their needs. When a child dies in these early years, the family is left with a sense of purposelessness. The child played an important role in the family. He or she may have been the family member who had been ill for so long that the family's life revolved around hospital appointments and prolonged periods of anxiety, or he or she may have been the child who was getting on fairly independently and successfully, but met with a fatal accident.

Now that the child has died, the family is forced to re-focus, and to find different meanings in life. Surviving siblings will be left with very mixed feelings. On the one hand, they may feel deep sorrow, fear and rage. On the other hand, there may be a feeling of relief which sets off guilt at the thought that they may have magically caused the sibling's death by some of their bad feelings. The problem with all of these ordinary reactions is that if they are not understood and talked about openly, the family is faced with insurmountable conflict made up of guilt, regret, fear and jealousy that has no access for expression.

Perhaps now it becomes clearer to see how much disorganization and distress occurs when a child dies. The family has to regroup and each member's roles must be readjusted. Mixed feelings abound, particularly unresolved sibling rivalries. To prevent further deterioration within the family, it is important to talk about what has happened and how it affects each family member and the family as a whole. This does not mean to say that the grief work will then be easy. The pain is inevitable. However, the long-term outcome for the survival of the family unit will be healthier, and the likelihood of each family member not being permanently disabled by the loss will be increased.

Each death has a unique significance to each of the bereaved, so that when talking about bereavement, some words will be wrong for some people. That's why so many people resist talking about their feelings. They worry that they are not doing it right, as if there is a right and a wrong way to feel.

When a parent dies at what is considered a reasonable age, so that they are thought to have had a 'good innings', adult children may find it difficult to acknowledge their grief. Having announced that one's parent has died, the question is often asked, "How old was the parent?" If the reply is seventy or over, the enquirer may sigh with relief as if to say that it is all right. But it's not all right. It is very painful to lose a parent, very sad. We want them to be there to share in the milestones in our lives and in our children's lives.

Some parents and children distance themselves from each other early in life, but it is a pity that people are not given enough time to grieve the deaths of their parents. Typically, a few days off work are all that is offered. People seem to be expected to carry on as if they have not just experienced one of the most painful events of a lifetime - the loss of a loved one.

Another painful aspect of parents' deaths has to do with the fact that the buffer between the adult child and his or her potential death has now been removed. As long as one's parents are alive, it feels as though one's own death is out of sight. For many people, this is the time when they most acutely sense their own mortality. It is not uncommon in grief, as has been mentioned earlier, for the bereaved to complain of the same symptoms the parents had. In a way this phenomenon symbolizes the bereaved person's own fear of dying.

The grief process has been discussed in general terms and it has been emphasized that it will differ for each individual. The death of a partner and the death of a child have been illustrated as examples of how close family members will usually be thrown into a state of disarray initially, gradually building a different kind of life following the bereavement, different because the bereaved will no longer play an active part in it, only the memories will survive. The death of an ageing parent has also been described.

It may be that the person who left an individual feeling bereaved was not a close family member, but a friend, a colleague, a neighbor, or even perhaps a public figure. There may be times when we are deeply affected by the loss of someone outside of the immediate family. It may be because of a special affection for the person, or perhaps the death reminds us of previous losses in our lives, and those old painful feelings may re-emerge each time we experience subsequent less immediate losses.

There are, of course, numerous ways in which people die. People regard **dying of old age** as a natural cause. Illnesses are more frequently seen in ageing people. Middle-aged people are susceptible to stress-related conditions such as coronary disease, ulcers, colitis, and cancer, to name a few. People may suffer from a particular condition for a large part of their life and die in old age. Others may die as soon as the condition strikes.

When a loved one dies suddenly, the bereaved will not have had time to do any preparatory grief work. During long illnesses, both the bereaved and the dying are able to go through the grief process together. However, that often does not happen. If one or both parties is unable to confront reality, denial will prevent movement through the grief process. In those cases, the bereaved may not differ at all from those who had been prepared.

People with HIV-related illnesses and their families are faced with a long-term condition that is particularly painful to go through. In addition to the physical deterioration, they are also faced with a lack of sympathy and condemnation on the part of a society which still knows little about the condition and isolates the individuals and their families, making it very difficult to cope with the distress.

There are so many ways to die, too many to discuss in a single chapter. In many ways, categorizing different ways of dying is unhelpful, because it masks individual differences and meanings inherent in a particular loss. For example, if Mrs. X and Mrs. Y both had husbands who committed suicide, their reactions and experience of their respective losses would not be the same. Some feelings may be strikingly similar due to the fact that both women grew up in the same society where a particular attitude was learned in response to suicide. Both women are likely then to experience society's disapproval of suicide, but over and beyond that the kind of relationship each had with her respective husband, the histories of these relationships and individual losses bear very little resemblance to each other's personal experience.

The death of a younger person is usually met with more alarm than the death of someone who is old. Whenever death is unexpected it is difficult for the survivor to quickly adjust to the sudden life change. **Accidents** account for a large proportion of sudden deaths. The grief process for those who survive tends to be longer and more difficult in these circumstances. Understandably, disbelief lasts longer and the reality of the death is not accepted as quickly as those deaths which were anticipated because of illness.

The survivor may not have been present at the time of the accident. People are killed in accidents on the road, rail, in the air and at sea, to name a few. The survivor is informed by an authority figure of the death.

Most survivors report that they never forget the words used informing them of their loved one's death, the words which come as a total blow. Not having been present at the scene of the accident creates many unanswerable questions for the survivors. They want to know how the accident could have been avoided. Whose fault was it? Did the victim suffer? Was the death instant or prolonged? Was there any help?

It can take a long time before the urgency of these questions lessens, letting the fact of the death become clearer. It is not uncommon in these circumstances for survivors to recognize their loved one in the street and to run towards them, only to find they misperceived the passer-by. The telephone rings and is answered excitedly with the expectation that the one who died has telephoned to say it was all a terrible mix-up. The doorbell rings, and again hopes are dashed when a next-door neighbor appears instead of the wished for loved one. Similarly, handwriting on envelopes can be misidentified leading to the expectation of a letter from him or her. All of these reactions are likely to occur to a much lesser extent when the death was anticipated.

It is important for the survivor to talk about the accident and his or her feelings about it. Most people can talk about the facts of the accident and may go over the details again and again. While that is a useful part of understanding what has happened, it will not be truly helpful unless the survivor can also describe the associated feelings he or she has.

We live in a society which discourages people from spelling out their feelings, the implication being that feelings are implicit in what we say. In my view this attitude leads to confusion, miscommunication, isolation, and a less healthy approach to living. Feelings need to be made explicit. Each person will have a unique mixture of feelings in response to life events. Opposite feelings can exist simultaneously, since they are not governed by rules. Logic has no place in one's emotional experience. Creativity comes from one's emotional base. The ability to get in touch with one's feelings, without imposing rationale and rules, does not come easily to everyone. It is a skill worthy of practice since many inner resources lie hidden in that part of the human mind.

We can only know how another person feels if we allow him or her to communicate that to us. For example, if a man whose wife died in a road

87

accident told me he felt depressed, it would be a mistake for me to believe I understood how he was feeling. What is evident is that he has identified his depressed mood. He will, however, have different sets of feelings that also need to be acknowledged. Therefore, I would say to him that he feels depressed right now. That is one set of reactions he has had to his wife's death and I would add that there may be a variety of feelings in addition to feeling depressed. In that way I invite him to reflect on the way he feels and to explore further his reaction to his loss. It would not be helpful to say, "Yes, of course you're depressed. But you're still young enough. You'll remarry and get on with your life eventually." That kind of statement precludes any further exploration of feelings. In fact, the implicit message is, "Please don't talk about your emotions. I can't bear to get in touch with your pain, nor do I wish to get too close to you."

If the listener begins to understand the survivor's feelings, barriers are gradually lowered, deepening the level of communication. The survivor can then speak more honestly about his or her life and the meaning of the loss. A survivor can only lower defensive barriers if the listener seems to be trustworthy. After all, the very purpose of these barriers is to protect one's self from the emergence of painful thoughts, ideas, and feelings. If no defences existed each of us would be overwhelmed by a barrage of memories, conflicts, wishes, and ideas. In order to function, only a certain degree of awareness can be tolerated at any given time. This is not to say that it is unhealthy to lower defences in the company of a trusted person. On the contrary, that can increase the meaningfulness in understanding what is being experienced.

Thus, the survivor asks himself, "Can I trust this person enough to reveal my vulnerable self without fear of being judged, attacked, ridiculed, or misunderstood?" Most misunderstandings occur because the listener has only taken in what the survivor has been able to say. The survivor's nonverbal communications may have been ignored.

For example, as the man talked about his depression, in the earlier example, he may have made gestures which clearly indicated frustration at not understanding how all of this could have happened. He may have shrugged, thrown open his arms, tapped his foot, or looked at the listener with a questioning expression in his eyes. Providing the listener grasped these communications, he or she would have been in a position to say to the survivor, "You're telling me how depressed you feel. As you have been talking to me, I have also sensed your frustration. Even the expression on your face seemed to be asking, 'How could this have happened to her?

Why?' Perhaps you are feeling frustrated as well as more generally depressed at the moment. I'm not sure." If the listener was accurate, the survivor might then verbalize his frustration, and the listener might have been surprised to hear how much the survivor had to say about it.

By acknowledging a feeling that the survivor was having trouble with, resulting in it only being communicated through gestures and facial expression, the listener facilitated the way for the survivor to verbalize all the frustrations that had been building up inside, and allowed him to move forward through the grief process. Had the listener's comment about frustration been inaccurate, the survivor would have said so, and would have continued to talk about his depression. Either way, the listener let the survivor know that it was all right to explore and express feelings. When people keep a stiff upper lip, closeness, helpfulness, and caring are strictly limited. While it is useful to carry out practical tasks for those in mourning, it is not enough.

What makes so many people afraid of hearing about painful feelings? It seems to have to do with how much one has explored one's own feelings. If the listener has never done any self-exploration, he or she is bound to feel out of depth when hearing another person express painful feelings. The individual is demonstrating an ability to introspect in a way the listener never has. The experience will be unnerving and will arouse uncomfortable feelings within the listener, such as feelings of fear, inadequacy, apprehension, and perhaps sadness - feelings that had not up until now been recognized.

The following dialogue exemplifies the kind of listening and responding that I recommend to encourage the expression of another person's feelings:

SURVIVOR: *Since my wife died over a year ago I've lost interest in most things I used to do. Most of the time I feel like I'm going through the motions of life aimlessly. (Pause). You must think I'm feeling sorry for myself. Most of my friends have stopped contacting me. They're probably fed up with me as well. People expect me to pull myself together and get on with my life. I miss Fran so much. (Fighting back tears, pause). I feel depressed most of the time.*

LISTENER: *You've told me how you've lost interest in most of the activities you enjoyed before Fran died. You said that you seem to, well, I* *think you put it this way, that you feel like you're going through the motions of life aimlessly.*

SURVIVOR: *On weekends, Fran and I would get the household chores out of the way on Saturdays. And in the afternoons she'd meet up with her friends and do things they liked to do, and I'd go to the ball game with one or two of the guys. In the evening we'd take it easy and talk about our plans and hopes for our teenage children. We had so much to look forward to. Sometimes we agreed. (Chuckles). Many times we disagreed. I used to get annoyed with her, but . . . We had some terrible rows. You know, about money and . . . Well, I didn't exactly get on with her parents. There were a lot of problems. But I knew who I was then. Now I feel lost, and there doesn't seem to be any point in anything any more. (Puts his hands over his face).*

LISTENER: *(Pause). It sounds like you're saying that since Fran's death your life has drastically changed. You were telling me how you used to spend your Saturdays. Part of the day you did things together, and in the afternoons you pursued your own interests. You've told me how your friends have distanced themselves from you. It sounds like they find it difficult to stand by you while you're feeling depressed, purposeless, and unsure of who you are. (Pause).*

SURVIVOR: *(Nods silently, deep in his thoughts).*

LISTENER: *One thing you said struck me particularly because I don't think it's easy while grieving to remember the rows and the disagreements without feeling guilty or frightened, or all kinds of mixed feelings. It sounds like Fran was taken away from you so suddenly that you never had time to resolve some of your differences.*

SURVIVOR: *Don't get me wrong. Our marriage was okay. We used to argue, but I don't want you to think we were going to break up or anything like that.*

LISTENER: *Sure.*

SURVIVOR: *But I keep going over the rows we used to have. And I said some mean things to her. Sometimes I called her names. And I just want to tell her how much I love her, how much I miss her. (Pause). I keep feeling it's my fault that she was killed. If only*

> *I'd gone out to do the shopping that morning instead of her,*
> *then she'd never have been run down by that driver.*

LISTENER: *There are so many feelings and thoughts going round and round*
your head. I can hear your frustration and distress.

The dialogue above serves to demonstrate a facilitative interaction. The listener gave no false reassurance and enabled the survivor to get more in touch with his feelings and begin to move through the grief process as he put some of his confused and contradictory feelings into words.

It is important to distinguish true reassurance from false reassurance. True reassurance is best communicated by the reassurer's presence. Being there, and allowing the bereaved to experience their pain without concern for us is really supportive and reassuring. False reassurance usually takes the form of minimizing and trivializing the tragedy, telling the bereaved they will have forgotten all about it soon. False reassurance pushes the bereaved to pretend they are all right *for our sake*. In other words, the recipient of true reassurance is the bereaved, while the recipient of false reassurance is the one who falsely reassures and goes away feeling much better, leaving the bereaved feeling misunderstood, hurt, and helpless.

Simply being there, in a non-intrusive way, standing by conveying an attitude which includes sensitivity, caring, warmth, respect and concern, is most appreciated by those who are temporarily feeling as if they are no longer part of the world. Such presence breaks that isolation. Being available with some frequency helps, and friends and relatives are usually best placed to provide that kind of support. For example, telephoning at frequent and regular intervals initially may help the bereaved individual, couple, or family, feel like they are establishing a new routine. The incoming telephone call might become part of that routine and the contact can sometimes help motivate them to reorganize, to move forward in the grief process.

There are so many ways to live one's life and so many ways to die. Those who mourn for loved ones who committed *suicide* often experience a particularly complicated grief process. People attending the funeral find it hard to know what to say because they are perplexed and feel rejected by the deceased. The bereaved in these circumstances often feel a sense of shame, as if it were their fault that their loved one chose to die.

Grief work is complicated by the mixture of anger and guilt. The bereaved are angry at the person who died for deliberately creating this situation. They feel guilty because they believe that they should have known, that they should have been able to recognize their loved one's distress or alleviate it.

These cruel remarks from people who were not in a position to understand what had gone on in recent years, severely hamper the grieving process. Most of the literature indicates that suicide survivors find it very difficult to get over their feelings of guilt even though it was not their fault. It seems that the guilt is intensified by society's attitude that there must have been something very wrong with a family where a member took his or her own life.

Children of a parent who committed suicide are considered to be at high risk, by some researchers, for also committing suicide. In order to reduce that probability, these survivors need to be able to work through their feelings in an attempt to go on living. When a parent's action indicates that life is not worth living, a loyal child may feel obligated to that parent to join him or her.

The survivor who chooses to go on living is left with the disappointment at times of joy and success that the parent chose not to live to see it, leaving him or her with intense feelings of anger as well as guilt. A common self-criticism people experience has to do with not often enough having told their loved ones who committed suicide that they loved them.

In this chapter, I have briefly described a variety of factors surrounding grief work. It has not been possible to write with the same intensity as the pain felt by the bereaved and those supporting them. The reality has been understated because the approach has been a general one.

The chapter has been worthwhile if it has shown that a mixture of contradictory reactions to the loss of a loved one is not cause for alarm. Most importantly, all of this has been worthwhile if it has enabled readers to more readily accept that dying is an important part of living. It can be incorporated into our lives so that it is not split off and only confronted at times when people close to us die, and when we near our own deaths. If we remove the taboo to the topic of death, we can talk about it more openly and work through our related fears and anxieties together.

Fairy tales end with the words, " . . . and they all lived happily ever after." Perhaps it would be more appropriate in this more realistic context to end with the words, " . . . *and we survived the deaths of those close to us. Gradually, we reorganized our lives adapting to our new circumstances. We learned to accept the fact of our loss. We never got over it, but we managed to live with it.*"

Each of us is unique. Many factors will determine how the rest of our lives will be. Although someone dear has gone, not all has been lost, and we are entitled to our hopes for the future.

CHAPTER
N I N E

Why is the Psychotherapeutic relationship different *from all other relationships?*

There are questions to be answered about a relationship where one party is engaged as a counselor or psychotherapist and the other party - an individual, couple, family, or group, known as the client - seeks to improve ways of being in relationships. In other relationships there is mutuality, but here the focus is on the emotional development of only one party - the client. In other relationships we do not have to always meet in the same place and limit our interactions to a definite length of time. However, in the psychotherapeutic relationship the sessions begin and end on time for a specified length of time.

In other relationships we are not expected to say everything that comes to mind - ideas, feelings, and thoughts that we have neither examined nor censored, yet in the psychotherapeutic relationship, the client is encouraged to stay in touch with fleeting thoughts and feelings long enough to put them into words, so that both parties have the opportunity of staying more deeply in touch with the client's inner world.

The answer is, "Because we were *slaves* to our less conscious motivations until it was recognized that *freedom* to gain more control of them was possible through understanding the mental contents of emotional life. That freedom came from self-exploratory work within the framework of a relationship which was, of necessity, *different* from other relationships."

Creating the Setting Most Conducive to Start Work on One's Emotional Development

It is for the counselor or psychotherapist to create a nonjudgmental atmosphere so that the client can feel safe to self-explore. Rogers (1957) talked about this feature of the relationship as *acceptance of the client.* In my work I prefer not to ask questions, and I have found this to be the most effective way of not being perceived as judgmental. Questions put people on the spot. Any time a counselor feels the impulse to ask a question, if he or she silently converts the question into a statement, in that very short time span clients typically continue uninterrupted with material far more meaningful to them than the answer to the counselor's question would have been.

However, many clients welcome the opportunity to respond to questions with detailed, intellectualized accounts of their lives. Others deal with the anxiety produced by questions by doing their best in their responses and wondering what the 'right' answers are. Either way, the nonjudgmental setting cannot tolerate a questioning approach coming from the counselor's frame of reference. It is important to see the world from clients' frames of reference, rather than pressurizing them to alter their presentation on account of the counselor's impatience. This is one area where the absence of questions can enhance the counselor's acceptance of the client.

Langs (1982) advocated the following ground rules for both psycho-therapy and psychoanalysis: (a) a set fee, hour, and length of sessions; (b) the use of free association; (c) the absence of physical contact and other extratherapeutic gratifications; (d) the therapist's relative anonymity; (e) physicianly concern; (f) the use of neutral interventions geared primarily toward interpretations; and (g) an exclusive one-to-one relationship with total confidentiality. Langs (1975) believed that the patient utilized the therapist's management and maintenance of the ground rules, "as a basis for unconscious, incorporative identification. Constructively handled, it provides a basis for positive and adaptive inner change that supplements the patient's endeavors to achieve conflict resolution and symptom relief through cognitive insight based on the therapist's interpretations".

The ground rule of confidentiality in psychotherapy had its origin in the Hippocratic Oath and, later, became coded in non-medical psychotherapeutic professions (e.g. in the UK, The British Psychological Society and The British Association for Counselling. Freud (1963) recommended confidentiality as one of the rules of analysis. Later analysts developed Freud's meanings of the rules in terms of *setting boundaries* for the treatment setting. They drew attention to the therapeutic hold that these rules provided for the patient, so that the rules were seen on the one hand to define the therapeutic relationship and, later, they were perceived as tools that provided the patient with a sense of safety in a consistent and secure setting (Greenacre, 1971; Langs, 1976; and

Winnicott, 1965). Adherence to the ground rules, particularly that of confidentiality, sets standards for psychotherapists and can be carried out so as to convey respect and the wish to be professionally helpful to those served (Delroy, 1984).

The relationship is crucial because interpersonal relationships are of prime importance in anyone's individual psychological functioning. Indeed, our earliest tasks in life prepare us for the multitude of relationships we will be faced with throughout our lives. The consequences of these relationships with relatives, friends, employers, teachers, clergymen, storekeepers, *etc.* will have much to do with our total personality adjustment. It is, after all, an observation and assessment of our client's interpersonal relationships that permit us to better understand their intrapsychic processes, deeper realms of consciousness, attitudes and motivations. These factors help to explain how the psychotherapeutic relationship is of primary importance as a tool in any therapeutic treatment plan and as the curative agent to be used in providing for the client a *corrective emotional experience* (Alexander, French et al. 1946).

Before elaborating on the psychoanalytic, behavioral, and humanistic orientations in terms of the changes that will hopefully occur, I feel that some brief space must be devoted to some of the concepts developed by Margaret Mahler. My understanding of the naturalness of the *relationship* playing a central role in therapy has developed from my appreciation of some of her thoughts. It is the process of being totally merged with the mother, to becoming a separate individual, and then relating back to others as a separate entity, that strikes me as such a huge task.

The infant comes into the world totally unaware of his or her separateness which has suddenly been thrust upon him or her. The first few months of life are spent in gradually coming to some *dim faint awareness* that many of the infant's needs are being satisfied by an external caretaking agent. The symbiotic phase is one where the infant perceives his or her relationship with the caretaker as one of a *dual unity within a common boundary*. In order for the *separation-individuation* phase to ensue satisfactorily, the infant has to initially experience body differentiation from the caretaker, secondly a specific bond with the caretaker, and in addition, close proximity of the caretaker while the infant develops the autonomic functions of the ego apparatus. Only after the foregoing has been established can the infant begin to relate (Mahler, 1975).

It is my respect and adherence to the rules of psychoanalysis that stop me from taking on board the person-centered approach *in toto*. I have made it clear how valuable most of Rogers' concepts are. Unfortunately, there seems to be ambiguity in what he had to say about respecting the separateness of people who come to us for person-centered growth work. He, and other person-centered therapists, do not appear to have well-defined boundaries (Mearns and Thorne, 1988; Rogers, 1961).

Person-centered therapists set few limits on the relationship. For example, starting on time and ending on time may or may not happen. Clients may be told that they have *about* an hour. Anonymity is not important to person-centered therapists either. Clients may be burdened with lots of personal information about the therapist. There are some person-centered therapists who feel okay about having physical contact with clients - a hug, or a reassuring hand on the client's shoulder, arm, or leg. As far as I am concerned, a hug, or a hand on a client's arm or shoulder, usually represents false reassurance. Rather than facilitating someone's inner exploration, it is likely to put the person back in touch with the outer world, encouraging conscious ideas and daydreams about the counselor's process as well as providing pathological gratification instead of deeper levels of emotional insight.

Rogers (1961) did say we should keep in mind our clients' separateness. However, present day person-centered therapy could be viewed as seductive. What is most worrying about that is that the counselors do not see it that way. Therefore, they may not be recognizing some iatrogenic consequences they may be causing for their clients. Being seductive towards people who want to work on their emotional development, in my view, disregards their needs for autonomy and independence, encouraging them instead to merge with the therapist, increasing the likelihood of leaving people with unresolved positive transferences.

There are person-centered therapists who appear to have difficulty in believing that it would be harmful to make love to clients for whom they have loving feelings, since, as far as they are concerned, this is what being true to one self means. Reputable person-centered therapists do not make love to their clients, but apart from Codes of Ethics placed on them by professional bodies, my impression is that some of them are not sure why they don't. I am not suggesting that person-centered therapists are using clients for their own sexual satisfaction. I am emphasizing that seductiveness does not have to have as its goal sexual relations, but it does set out to win others' affection. I see this as an abuse of power. In emotional growth work, clients have not come in order to learn how to idealize or even be fond of another person. Self-knowledge is what they seek and this can only succeed, in my opinion, if the therapist sets clear limits on the relationship. Otherwise people may remain in person-centered therapy for most of their lives because they only feel okay in that atmosphere. The work is never completed.

In other words, a client who may have idealized significant people in his or her life runs the risk in person-centered therapy of working through issues about negative feelings towards significant people, but repeating strong positive feelings in relation to the counselor without gaining any insight into the meanings belonging to those positive feelings. If relationship issues are played out without being understood, then in my view nothing therapeutic is occurring. *Feel-good therapy*, which includes touchey-feeley interactions between therapists and clients, often only has short-term effects, like behavior therapy and drug therapy. What *feel-good* therapy, behavior therapy, and drug therapy have in common is that they all depend solely on positive reinforcement to maintain levels of feeling okay, but once the positive reinforcement is withdrawn the feelings often dissipate.

Ground rules were established in psychoanalysis by Freud (1963), and later used to serve as a framework for clients to work in (Milner, 1976), where they could feel safe to discover more about themselves, feeling secure that therapists would manage the boundaries, thereby maintaining the framework, reducing the risk of a chaotic and countertherapeutic relationship. Unfortunately, my view of person-centered therapy is that it is for the most part being practised in the chaotic way I have described. Perhaps that is why in the UK one rarely finds qualified clinical psychologists, social workers, psychiatrists, and psychotherapists from recognized training institutes calling themselves person-centered therapists.

In psychoanalytic, behavioral, and humanistic therapy, the relationship is used to facilitate change in the client in the following ways:

Psychoanalytic Psychotherapy

One first thinks of the *transference neurosis* in the context of psychoanalytic treatment (Freud, 1963). While this is of crucial importance in the therapeutic relationship, Langs (1982) has described quite systematically additional factors that strengthen the possibility of the client successfully experiencing personality change. Others in the field share many of his conclusions and techniques to varying degrees. He has, however, written about them more extensively.

Before elaborating upon the work of Langs, I would like to point out that the transference issue has been an understandably loaded one in the history of psychoanalysis. Fromm-Reichmann (1950) and Otto Will (1959) stressed the importance of *relatedness* as the key to successful therapy with schizophrenics. Many others stressed the importance of counter-transference as interference in the psychoanalytic procedure (Kvarnes, 1976; Searles, 1959).

Langs (1973) advocated conducting psychoanalytic psychotherapy within a consistent framework where the *ground rules* were made clear and explicit at the outset. The therapist's task is to listen to the manifest and latent content in terms of the adaptive and therapeutic contexts. Very carefully the communicative therapist attends to transference and counter-transference issues as they arise so that they may be worked through promptly, facilitating the client's insight and emotional correction. Langs (1978) emphasized that it is only by carefully listening to the client that the therapist can successfully identify a bridge whereby an interpretation of the close derivative meanings can be made providing the client with genuine, emotional insight. The client will hopefully confirm the interpretation by deepening his or her process and producing fresh and new material. And so the process continues until the client experiences symptom alleviation. There will be times when the client will not confirm the therapist's interpretations. Such an outcome indicates to the therapist the need to listen to the client so that the client can get back on track, and the therapist, through careful listening and using bridges, may yet make correct interpretations.

Where the therapist fails to listen, becomes defensive and is not genuine, an iatrogenic syndrome will develop. Countertransference issues that are not resolved in therapy can produce pathological vicious circles. The relationship in psychoanalytic psychotherapy is necessary so that an other, the therapist, can listen, make interpretations, and be genuinely concerned about the client's psychological health.

Behavior Therapy

In a behavioral framework one has to first differentiate radical (Skinner, 1971) from more cognitively-oriented behaviorism (Lazarus, 1981) before getting into any discussion of the therapeutic relationship. Stimulus-response theory would use a machine for a therapist (e.g. programmed instruction), so I will address my remarks in this section with those behaviorists in mind who base therapy upon the relationship (e.g. Wilson and Evans, 1976; Goldfried and Davison, 1976; and Meichenbaum, 1977).

In order to set up a behavioral treatment program with a client, a trusting mutually respectful, honest and direct relationship is essential. Many people are still surprised when they hear behaviorists say so. It is hard for therapists of other orientations to accept a behaviorist as being warm, sympathetic, humane and non-controlling.

In a behavioral framework, empathy, respect, unconditional positive regard and the therapist's genuineness in the therapeutic relationship are fundamental and necessary for therapy to evolve. However, unlike Rogers' person-centered therapy, they are not considered sufficient. The development of rapport is very important. The key to success in behavior therapy revolves around a correct and accurate description of the client's behavior to be changed. It is not the therapist who chooses the behavior to be targeted but the client.

Through the relationship the client can explore the antecedents, behaviors, consequences and organismic variables that are maintaining the targeted behaviors. Such exploration will often include the revelation of past experiences as well as the client's attitudes, biases, motivations and personal habits. One is only likely to make oneself known to another in a *safe* relationship. Many behavioral techniques require the client's cooperation and trust. For example, in teaching a client the techniques of deep relaxation in preparation for systematic desensitisation, or for its own value, the client must at least have some feeling of calm in relation to the therapist. Interestingly enough, behavior therapy has some built-in techniques for establishing rapport. For example, *contracting* is an excellent method for entering a relationship where the client can see what he or she can expect of the therapist and treatment and *vice versa*.

The mere process of contracting emphasizes the mutual respect inherent in the relationship as well as the honesty and directness of the approach. A major factor in terms of developing the relationship is the concept of control. In order for behavior therapy to be effective the client must appreciate that it is the client and not the therapist who is in control. The client can stop any procedure at any given time, or start a new one. Behavior therapy that recognizes the importance of a good relationship usually makes this control issue explicit in the contract, yet dispelling another myth. In addition, behaviorists use home visits, phone calls and other aspects of the relationship to serve as positive reinforcers in modifying specific behaviors. Thus it can be seen that behavior therapy combines elements of the psychoanalytic and humanistic-experiential therapies in the use it makes of the therapeutic relationship.

Person-Centered Therapy

I have chosen Carl Rogers' person-centered therapy to serve as the prototype for experiential-humanistic psychotherapy in this discussion. In his paper describing the six necessary and sufficient conditions for personality change (Rogers, 1957), the first condition is that two persons are in psychological contact. The following conditions are all derived from the first: the client is in a state of incongruence, feeling vulnerable or anxious. The incongruence has to do with his or her organismic experience differing somehow from the self-concept. The therapist, on the other hand, is integrated in the relationship, in a state of congruence - that is, genuine, freely and truly himself or herself. The therapist has unconditional positive regard for the client, always aware of the client's positive ongoing process, moving toward maturity. The therapist experiences and communicates to the client an empathic understanding of the client's experience. The therapist senses the client's private world as if it were his or her own.

Here lies the crux! If the client, at least partially receives (perceives) the therapist's communications of unconditional positive regard and empathic understanding of the client then the conditions for beginning the process of personality change have been met. The importance of the client's perception of the therapist in relation to him or her is paramount. It is only when one feels confirmed by another as existing and having feelings, that one can then deepen one's experience and grow (Rogers, 1957). Rogers central hypothesis of person-centered therapy was:

> *It is that the individual has within himself or herself vast resources for self-understanding, for altering his or her self-concept, attitudes, and self-directed behavior - and that these resources can be tapped if only a definable climate of facilitative psychological attitudes can be provided (In Kutash and Wolf, 1986).*

Rogers (1957) went on to summarize the three core conditions - empathy, congruence and unconditional positive regard which apply in any situation in which the development of the person is a goal. These core conditions have largely contributed to my development as a psychotherapist. I attribute much importance to them and subsequently endeavor to pass them on to the many health professionals and educators who attend my counseling skills courses. The way I work with these concepts is not completely faithful to person-centered therapy, since as I have already stated, I am essentially a psychoanalytic psychotherapist who appreciates the importance of the core conditions which underlie the person-centered approach. I teach them in the following way:

Congruence - the here-and-now

The first condition I introduce is congruence, and for me it is the most challenging concept to convey to beginning counselors and therapists. I talk about it initially in terms of the here-and-now; it comes up later when I go through Rogers (1957) necessary and sufficient conditions for therapeutic personality change, and again when I talk about the importance of the counselor being sensitive to his or her own experiencing. In this way, I am able to talk about it on three occasions within three separate lectures, reinforcing the importance of the need for the counselor to be aware of what is going on in the relationship, so as to reduce the likelihood of passing on his or her psychopathology to the client by attributing to the client his or her own unresolved conflicts. I use the concept of congruence liberally, so as to explain in non-psychoanalytic language concepts of transference and countertransference, since it translates so well.

Staying with the here-and-now is what differentiates a counseling or psychotherapy session from a social chat. Here-and-now phenomena have to do with how the client and therapist are experiencing each other in the psychotherapy relationship, and the therapist's ability to remain aware of here-and-now material so that it can be acknowledged and kept available, rather than shoved under the carpet as often happens in non-therapeutic daily interactions.

Most people are taught from an early age not to deal with the here-and-now. Teaching children good manners has often included educating them to behave in an opposite way to how they feel. As we developed, we became experts at distancing ourselves from our true feelings so as not to make waves or appear argumentative. That is why it is difficult for many people later on in life to get back in touch with their feelings. They have been suppressed for so long, it is often difficult to identify them. Let me offer an example to clarify this important issue.

An old friend visits, and you are really pleased to see her. You spend a lively half-hour together catching up on recent news when your friend makes a personal remark that disturbs you. Your initial reaction may be to tell yourself that you must have misheard her and you begin to convince yourself that you have a hearing problem. During these few seconds that have passed since the remark, your friend is happily chatting away so that you dismiss the hurtful remark and once again begin to enjoy her company.

Ten minutes later another disturbing personal remark is made, and almost reflexively you find yourself inquiring as to whether you can get your guest something to drink. Prior to her response, you find yourself busying yourself over preparation of coffee, again wondering to yourself why she makes unpleasant personal jibes. Returning from the kitchen with a tight smile, you pass your friend some coffee and are so relieved when you find yourself chattering away about some amusing incident so that both of you can *turn away* from what is going on between you, and just when you are again feeling relaxed and comfortable with her, she does it again.

As a last resort you merely change the subject and begin to transmit signs that it is getting late and display less interest in her conversation in the hope that she will leave. She does leave and you tell each other how good it was getting together again. You say it like you really mean it. This is not because you are a liar. It is because you also believe it at the moment you are saying it, because it would be too complicated to stay in touch with how uncomfortable she made you feel while you are saying your fond 'Good-byes'. She disappears down the road.

What happens next? Sometimes what happens next is you pick up the telephone and speak to a good friend and say, "You won't believe what that woman said to me today. She came over for a visit and she made these really snide remarks. Can you imagine?" Instead of letting people know at the time that their remarks are hurtful, or asking for more information in an assertive way, we often prefer not to address what is going on in the here-and-now, but get on the telephone to a third party and tell them about the 'there-and-then.'

Counselors and psychotherapists need to recognize their clients' strong emotional reactions to them *at the time*. The emotions can then be acknowledged, explored, and better understood *within* the sessions, rather than shoved under the carpet in a way that serves to repeat what goes on in less healthy relationships. In counseling and psychotherapy, the opportunity exists to create a relationship in which one can be true to oneself, and that can give clients the confidence to try it out in relationships outside the therapy room, so as to gain more satisfaction from those relationships and feel better about themselves.

The here-and-now is so important, the following example shows one way it can be attended to in a counseling session:

CLIENT: *(Has been attending weekly counseling sessions on Tuesdays with the counselor for the past four months. **The sessions have begun on time**. He arrives a few minutes early for his 2:00 pm appointment.*

Usually the counselor appears promptly to greet him. This week there is no sign of the counselor at 2:00 pm.

*The client commences on a checking process while he waits. **After a few seconds** he reaches for his diary to make sure he has come on the agreed day, and at the same time checks that it is Tuesday. The counselor's lateness results in the client questioning whether or not he is oriented. Self-doubt sets in quickly when significant people in our lives let us down. Now that the client is certain that he is there on the usual day and time and that the counselor said nothing about cancelling his session or being late, he attempts to put himself at ease by convincing himself that the counselor will arrive at any moment.*

*So far, **one and a half minutes have passed** and the client has felt most uneasy. As he waits he wonders whether the counselor is ill or absent from work. Perhaps the people on reception failed to tell him. Then he wonders if the counselor has met with some accident.*

***Two and a half minutes have elapsed**. The client becomes vaguely aware of feelings of irritation and annoyance. He wonders if the counselor is with another client or colleague, someone more important, and has forgotten the time because of not really caring about him and not wanting to work with him.*

***Three and a half minutes have now passed** and the thoughts and fantasies become more and more unpleasant. Suddenly the counselor appears.)*

COUNSELOR: *Hello, I'm sorry I kept you waiting.*

CLIENT: *(Client beams. He is so relieved to see the counselor and instantly suppresses the painful feelings he has experienced during the previous few minutes). Hello. Oh, that's no problem.*

(They walk silently to the counselor's office and seat themselves).

It's been quite an interesting week for me. Some difficult situations, and, er, others that were quite encouraging . . .

Now the session has begun the client may not spontaneously talk about his feelings about the counselor's lateness. The relief that was evident when he saw the counselor arrive may have the opposite effect. The last thing he would perhaps wish to dwell on was the disturbance that occurred at 2:00 pm due to the counselor's absence when the session was due to begin.

The client may engage in relating material that seems insightful and interesting. It would be *so easy for both of them to forget* about the initial disturbance in their counseling relationship that day. However, the counselor has as his responsibility the task of keeping it in his mind, so at some appropriate point the incident can be acknowledged.

It is important to appreciate that counselors decide to keep their errors in mind. Otherwise they will unconsciously leak out, resulting in sending veiled messages which will be confusing and countertherapeutic. In ordinary relationships, people tend not to acknowledge in a straightforward way what is going on. Instead, we give and receive double messages, often resulting in feelings of confusion and anxiety.

Interestingly enough, the fact that someone has let another person down is often most nearly forgotten when the first person begins complaining about somebody else. In counseling sessions complaints about others, need to be heard as possible unconscious complaints about the counselor. Therefore, after approximately twenty minutes, the session described above may continue as follows:

CLIENT: *Sunday night was a total write-off for me. A friend of mine called me in the week and asked me to meet him in a pub we both know. To tell you the truth, I didn't really want to go, but we used to work together and he's OK, so I said I'd meet him. That was me trying to be "Mr. Nice-Guy" as usual. This guy didn't show up. I was really fed up. It turned out that he had forgotten about it because he had to take one of his kids to the hospital. It turned out to be nothing serious. But while I was waiting for him I started to feel sorry for myself and I felt myself slipping into self-pity, feeling lonely and depressed about my family living so far away and the fact that I still feel like an*

> *outsider   here   despite   being   married   with kids. . . .*

The client may have continued associating, talking about whatever came to mind. At some point though the counselor could intervene and go over what feelings the client had been in touch with during the session with some of the content, and he could include the way the session began:

COUNSELOR: *We began a few minutes late today because of my lateness. You've been telling me about some of the difficulties you faced over the last week, as well as some situations where you were pleased with the way you were and how you felt. Later in the session, you described how fed up and lonely you felt when an old friend let you down on Sunday night, because he took one of his kids to the hospital. You reflected on how vulnerable you feel so far from your wider family, although you're married with kids, and let's not forget that I, too, let you down today with my lateness, and perhaps that also contributed to some of the feelings you were describing. You said you make a big effort to meet people on time, even when you are not quite sure you want to be there, and perhaps in some less conscious way you were reacting to what goes on here between you and me.*

CLIENT: *When I spoke to my friend on the phone we made arrangements to meet again. And I'll probably show up here as usual next week, as well. (Laughs)*

COUNSELOR: *You want me to know that you're going to give both of us another chance, not only your friend but also me.*

CLIENT: *Yes, I think that is what I'm saying. . . .*

That was an example of working with the here-and-now. It is rarely dramatic. It is often gentle, respectful, meaningful and true. The here-and-now represents an openness to experience. It enables clients to continue the process of self-exploration, moving towards their selves who they truly are.

Congruence - being true to one self

Rogers' (1957) third necessary and sufficient condition of therapeutic personality change is that the therapist is congruent or integrated in the relationship. I prefer to think of it as being true to one self. It seems to me that the goals of self-exploration have to do with discovering ourselves at a deeper level - at least, just beneath the surface; and also, acquiring the ability to stay open to our experience, even when that experience does not correspond to how we would prefer to feel about self, other(s), or a particular situation.

Being true to one self does not allow for *deliberately* shoving under the carpet unacceptable thoughts, wishes and feelings. Therefore being true to one self is opposite to denying one's feelings. Notice that I emphasized that it does not allow for deliberate denial. Much of what we deny is the result of unconscious defensive processes. Those who prefer to be true to themselves often notice that they have entered into a position of denial, and are more likely to be able to give it up, sooner rather than later.

Rogers did not expect counselors and therapists to be congruent in all of their relationships; but it is a requirement when working in a psychotherapeutic relationship. How can counselors and therapists know if they are congruent in relationships with their clients? Being congruent can result from self-exploratory work in a psychotherapeutic relationship. The result of that work should protect each client from the likelihood of having the counselor's psychopathology projected on to him or her. That is why counselors and psychotherapists are encouraged to have extensive counseling or psychotherapy themselves. It can serve to monitor the emotional life of counselors and alert them to their current vulnerabilities so that they are less likely to unwittingly transmit them to clients.

In a subsequent chapter I will give examples that I use when I teach counseling skills to health and mental health professionals that can be very helpful in allowing them to monitor their own emotional reactions to clients. More particularly, my intent is to enable them to be true to themselves within the therapy relationship, whether they provide physiotherapy, occupational therapy, medical consultations, nursing or counseling.

Unconditional Positive Regard

Rogers' (1957) fourth condition of the necessary and sufficient conditions of therapeutic personality change was that the therapist experiences unconditional positive regard for the client. The most important element of unconditional positive regard is that it is a *nonjudgmental* characteristic of the helping relationship. The attitude that is being conveyed to the client is, "I care about you because you are human." It is the opposite of the *conditions of worth* that exist in the real world. In counseling and psychotherapy, a climate is deliberately created through its framework that is different from the outside world. In this setting judgment and advice have no place, because neither contributes to understanding the client's meanings that he or she is in the process of discovering in order to feel more integrated and resourceful in relationships.

It is a fact that clients are vulnerable to exploitation within what is meant to be a psychotherapeutic relationship. It is easy to see how this can happen faced with the reality that there are charlatans in all walks of life. There are also different levels of exploitation and while having sexual relations with a client is the most overt form of it, milder forms can also be very disturbing and countertherapeutic for clients. In order to develop these ideas, it is necessary to incorporate the first condition of the necessary and sufficient conditions of therapeutic personality change. It was that two persons are in psychological contact (Rogers, 1957).

Thus, it can be seen that the characteristics of a helping relationship include two persons who are in psychological contact and a therapist who experiences unconditional positive regard for the client. Do you begin to see why so many people say to their friends and relatives, "What do you want to go and see a counselor for?" and, "You don't need therapy. You can talk to me." The idea of someone being in therapy appears to be disturbing to a number of people. Mostly, I have decried that attitude, but let me at least in this section explain the possible origins of this fear or concern which may be quite understandable.

A consultation with a doctor is often over within ten to fifteen minutes. If it goes on longer than that, the patient is usually dressed and the doctor is giving the patient information and recommendations concerning the medical condition. In other words, patients may feel vulnerable and exposed for a much shorter length of time than the standard fifty minutes for a counseling or psychotherapy session when the client remains exposed for the full session. What is more, there are no screens to hide behind in counseling and psychotherapy. Instead, the client is attended to with as much care and concern as a newborn. The counselor or therapist better be trustworthy when creating an atmosphere where clients are likely, at least unconsciously, to be experiencing a regression which has been provoked by the therapeutic setting.

Why then is it so important for two people to be in psychological contact? Rogers did not have anything to say about this, since he considered it to be obvious that there had to be two people. I prefer to understand it in terms of early developmental psychology (Mahler, 1975). Each of us is born of a mother. That means that our initial experience of the world takes place within the context of a relationship. Physical and emotional development may take place amid the ongoing reactions of the significant people in the infant's life.

For example, an infant sits up for the first time and this development may be acknowledged with much joy and pleasure by others. The infant may get a sense of having created some excitement, and notices considerable telephone activity on her behalf with conversations announcing the successful beginning of a new developmental phase. The infant decides to sit up again and thus confirms the hypothesis that sitting up produces quite a reaction. Bingo! Here they go again. Lots of attention. The world is my oyster! And in this way, many infants develop; whereas for those less fortunate, who are deprived of feedback within a caring relationship, very often there is a failure to thrive.

It makes good sense then that when people choose to work on their emotional growth and development later on in life, it needs to take place within the context of a relationship. In many respects, the psychotherapeutic relationship resembles the early relationship with the caretaker, inasmuch as both parties have as their common goal the emotional development of one of them. I therefore assume that clients experience *regression* in response to the therapeutic setting and emotional climate which is specially created. In order to manage it, they need to be treated with considerable respect, in a nonpatronizing manner, so as not to inadvertently strengthen it, which may not be in their best interests.

The dilemma is that, on the one hand, there needs to be a climate of safety, caring and acceptance which can trigger off a regression; and on the other hand, clients need to feel in charge of the sessions to the extent that they can enter into a therapeutic alliance. Both parties share the responsibility of engaging in a collaborative effort to facilitate clients' self-exploration and personal growth. Through the counselor's attitude, a satisfactory balance can be sustained, so that clients feel contained within the therapeutic relationship to engage in the work.

Counselors often interact with clients at an intense, emotional and intimate level. Situations could arise where unscrupulous or naive counselors exercise considerable control over them, either knowingly or unknowingly. At worst, vulnerable clients in regressed states, might be persuaded to remove their clothes and embrace their counselors, with the promise that such activity would produce symptom relief. Similarly, clients can easily be persuaded into a long-term counseling relationship that is more gratifying for the counselor than them. Beware of counselors who rely on their clients to provide them with emotional gratification as a substitute for satisfactory relationships in their private lives. The appropriate rewards of the work for the counselor take the form of payment and job satisfaction. Rogers (1957) encouraged counselors to be in touch with liking their clients. I prefer counselors to like their clients less, so that they can understand them more. If we are sufficiently involved in the therapeutic challenge, there is not much room for liking or disliking, but ample space to help people be true to themselves.

Interacting with clients at an intense, emotional and intimate level is acceptable if it is done for the good of the client in a non-exploitative manner. Clients enter into therapy and counseling so as to learn more about the way they are in relationships. An atmosphere of intimacy is created within the context of a *professional* relationship for one reason and for one reason only. The client can then explore his or her private world, in safety, without the threat of the counselor altering the framework and ground rules. Confident that the counselor has discretion and can be trusted, the client feels that the boundaries are secure and that the counselor will intrude no more than a trusted companion jointly engaged in a delicate task; in this instance, the task of exploring *just beneath the surface.*

Empathy

Rogers' (1957) fifth condition of the necessary and sufficient conditions of therapeutic personality change was that the therapist experiences an empathic understanding of the client's internal frame of reference and endeavors to communicate this experience to the client. In the psychotherapeutic relationship, unlike many other relationships, it is important to try to understand what clients are describing in the context of their internal frame of reference. In other words, being empathic requires counselors and therapists to try to hear and visualize clients' communications as if we were hearing and seeing them through their ears and eyes rather than our own. We need to understand what it means to them, rather than what it might mean to us.

Rogers put it clearly when he stated, ". . . a deep empathic understanding which enables me to see his private world through his eyes." He discussed an empathic understanding in the following way:

> . . . *To sense the client's anger, fear, or confusion as if it were your own, yet without your own anger, fear, or confusion getting bound up in it, is the condition we are endeavoring to describe (Rogers, 1961).*

And in his paper, "What We Know About Psychotherapy - Objectively and Subjectively" he stated:

> . . . *When the therapist can grasp the moment-to-moment experiencing which occurs in the inner world of the client as the client sees it and feels it, without losing the separateness of his own identity in this empathic process, then change is likely to occur (Rogers, 1961).*

To Conclude

The psychotherapeutic relationship has been distinguished from ordinary ones, emphasizing the ground rules that provide the therapeutic framework. The use of the relationship within the three major models of psychotherapy has been described. Transference for psychoanalytic psychotherapists (Langs, 1978); contracting for behavior therapists; (Goldfried and Davison, 1976) and Rogers' (1957) core conditions - congruence, unconditional positive regard, and empathy - for person-centered counselors and therapists. The rationale for the importance of the relationship was offered with reference to Margaret Mahler's (1975) work on separation-individuation. The dangers of exploitation within the special relationship were also elaborated upon. Particular emphasis was placed on the usefulness to clients of working with the here-and-now in order to discover more rapidly what seems to be just beneath the surface.

Counseling Skills Training for Health and Mental Health Professionals

Over the last eight years health and mental health professionals from various disciplines have attended my short courses on counseling skills and assertiveness workshops. Community-based and hospital nurses, physiotherapists (physical therapists), and occupational therapists (recreational therapists) have comprised the majority of participants. They come from different types of settings including the whole spectrum of health and mental health care. I want to describe how I try to teach them to feel more confident in caring for people in distress.

Earlier in the book I emphasized the lack of attention to counseling skills training within various medically-related disciplines, and my belief that when patients attend health and mental health settings they assume that staff know more about psychological processes than is the case. With that in mind, I devised a five-day intensive counseling skills course to provide some psychological theoretical background, as well as skills, to health care providers. Each course is limited to ten, and some have gone ahead with as few as four or five health professionals. The course aims to sharpen listening skills and to increase awareness of the complexities involved in the two-way interaction between patient and therapist.

From the outset the course was well received. Participants seemed most appreciative of the opportunity to fully describe their work settings. Recurrent themes spontaneously emerge in almost every course. These themes revolve around participants' reports of lack of supervision and support in their respective workplaces, and feelings of inadequacy in responding to their patients' emotional distress. Most of them express a clear wish at the outset to increase their levels of confidence in response to their patients' emotions. Another common theme is the stress of taking home patients' difficulties, and the hope that they can learn to leave those concerns at work.

The most sensible approach seemed to be one where course participants learned how to listen to their patients, acknowledging the content and feelings. They practised communicating back to their patients what they had so far understood. By concentrating primarily on listening to what patients say, and resisting an interpretive approach, I have also been able to help them extend their awareness of here-and-now phenomena, so that they have begun to listen at deeper levels. Within a few days, it has been possible to teach psychologically naive health and mental health professionals to attend primarily to process rather than content. I teach them to be nondirective facilitators, attending to patients' internal frames of reference. In this way, their patients can get more in touch with their psychological processes.

During the course, when participants practise the counseling skills they are said to be in the counselor's chair, and when they volunteer to provide genuine material for brief counseling sessions they are said to be in the client's chair. The 'counselors' are discouraged from asking the 'clients' questions because, in my view, one cannot simultaneously ask a question and maintain an empathic stance in line with the client's internal frame of reference. Questions come from counselors' frames of reference and not their clients'.

Initially, many participants express concern about being with a client for any length of time without asking questions, giving advice and reassurance. By the third day of the course, however, more often than not, there seems to be a wave of relief based on the experience that clients actually prefer the opportunity to get in touch with themselves rather than to have their feelings evaluated by somebody else. In addition, participants are frequently pleasantly surprised to discover the qualitative changes in communication when questioning is either reduced or entirely eliminated. As health and mental health professionals gain confidence in responding with increased sensitivity to clients, I have observed that they seem to become more aware of their own inner processes, becoming increasingly involved in the process of learning about emotional life.

While course participants extend their awareness, I learn from them about their work. Many of them work with people who have suffered strokes, head injuries and degenerative diseases, and the terminally ill. Among health and mental health professionals working in these areas, more themes emerge. Many of them spontaneously express concerns about lack of team work and an absence of strategies for being truthful with patients about their conditions. They want to know how to answer patients who ask how long they have to live. Frequently, the problem has to do with the fact that the team is led by a medical consultant who has not been clear with the patient about diagnosis and prognosis and leaves the nursing staff, physiotherapists and occupational therapists to care for the patient on a daily basis, without having the freedom to speak the truth with them. Many medical consultants refuse to discuss the difficulties nurses, and other therapists, wish to report concerning the patient's right to more information about his or her condition.

These health and mental health professionals subsequently become more and more conflicted, because the medical consultant refuses to consider what is best for the patient. Most times, consultants withhold information from patients because they either have not come to terms with it themselves and fear their patients' distress, or they cannot bear to admit to themselves or others that they cannot predict recovery, so they ignore the emotional needs of the patients and those caring for them.

In the UK most medical consultants and other health and mental health professionals have not been in counseling or psychotherapy themselves. Therefore, the ignorance they have about their own emotional lives gets transmitted to their patients. Non-medical health and mental health professionals seem to be more aware of their need for personal therapy, but the medical community understands very little about it. The illness model dictates medical practitioners' thinking, so psychological aspects of functioning only come to mind when there is some obvious excessive anxiety, depression, or other emotional presenting symptoms which are within their repertoire of probable recognition.

My exposure to health and mental health professionals from numerous settings throughout the UK, Ireland, and other parts of the world, has increased my respect for the very important work that they do. Nurses and other non-medical practitioners attend to their patients' needs continuously throughout the day, and often nights too. They are highly skilled and competent in the very specialized procedures and therapeutic interventions they implement. Yet, very often their unending hard work and dedication is minimized. Frequently, medical practitioners exclude them from the decision-making process in terms of their patients' care. This scenario where health and mental health professionals are undermined by their medical colleagues is described to me repeatedly by course participants from all parts of the world.

The way some medical practitioners abuse their power causes immeasurable stress among staff and patients. The arrogance that is so often expressed makes working life in any health service at times intolerable. In my course, I help participants recover their self-respect as health and mental health professionals. Away from the work place, they are able to clearly identify its stressful components and sometimes consider more direct strategies to implement upon their return. I rarely hear complaints about patients being the cause of stress; it tends to be colleagues and management who are the source of most of the aggravation.

My five-day intensive counseling skills course is described below. However, it is important to remember that each group is unique. Therefore, I have arbitrarily selected the order and content of the sorts of topics frequently covered. What falls under Day 2 or subsequent days in this account may come up on any of the days in reality, or may not emerge at all because no two groups are the same. The flavor of the course content and process is nevertheless conveyed.

THE FIVE-DAY COURSE

Day 1

The course is not introductory, because the only people eligible to come are those already working with people in distress. In that way the composition of participants usually is comprised of people with mixed levels of counseling experience. The course is set up so that each person can move on from whatever is his or her starting point. Qualified counselors, clinical and educational psychologists, as well as unqualified counselors who work for public agencies in the voluntary sector, often participate together with occupational therapists, physiotherapists, and nurses from mental health and health settings.

The ground rules are set at the beginning of the course. Participants discover that we begin and end on time. They find that one hour lunches last for sixty minutes, and that fifteen minute breaks are over after a quarter of an hour. My experience has been that this adherence to boundaries has been appreciated, and has significantly contributed to the commitment each of us has made to the learning process. I have been struck by the cooperation shown by participants, and in particular their compliance with the ground rules that have been set up to facilitate learning.

The ground rule of confidentiality is usually established before people introduce themselves. Course participants are requested to maintain confidentiality to make it possible for each of them to explore their experiences of working in their respective settings freely. I also ask them beforehand to come prepared to talk about themselves when they volunteer to be 'the client' for skills practice so that they can give 'the counselor' valid feedback in terms of how his or her interventions were helpful and in what ways they were unhelpful.

There is a further request for confidentiality which may at first glance seem unusual. I ask course participants to restrain themselves from discussing material that came up when they were 'clients' during the times they socialize with each other, lunchtime and coffee breaks, unless the person to whom the material belonged wishes to discuss it informally. In this way, they are required to remember what was confidential and what was not before they speak, in the same way as we have to consider very carefully what aspects of our work we are free to discuss in our private lives without breaking confidentiality. Another reason for this request has to do with maintaining the group's primary identity as a *learning* group, rather than it becoming a *psychotherapy* group. I believe that the two processes are quite distinct from one another and am clear about not confusing one with the other. Yet, both of these distinct and separate processes are in their own ways therapeutic.

The introductions are very important in terms of setting the stage. It is crucial that participants experience the course as a place where they can acquire skills which are vital for effective health and mental health care. Just as they are taught over the five-days how to hear clients' communications, it is imperative that each of them is heard when describing individual hopes from the course within the context of their work settings. Each participant is given the same kind of attention it is hoped will subsequently be made available to his or her patients.

People are usually apprehensive when they begin a new course, whether they are course leaders or participants. That apprehension provides the energy to facilitate the creation of a very special learning environment. I endeavor to sensitize course participants to the importance of allowing space for that apprehension to make itself known to them each time they encounter a new patient so as to be more sensitive to the patient's apprehension about being in an unfamiliar setting and, again, to facilitate the creation of an environment conducive to physical and emotional health.

It is my task during the first day to impart a great deal of background information specifically on person-centered theory and therapy, before beginning the skills practice proper. Sixty per cent of the first day includes references to developmental psychology, personality theories, psychopathology, and background to the person-centered approach. In this way, course participants are shown how important it is to be acquainted with psychological theory before setting up as a counselor.

The need for counselors to have personal therapy

Throughout this first day of the course emphasis is placed on the meaning of congruence, acknowledging here-and-now material and the responsibility of being true to oneself within the counseling relationship so as to avoid driving clients crazy. In other words, if counselors are unaware of themselves and their inner worlds, they are unlikely to be equipped to facilitate their clients' emotional development. In view of the fact that most of the course participants have not been in personal therapy, I alert them to commonplace situations which might suggest that their own psychological processes are interfering with the counseling process.

I ask participants to notice in their work when they spend considerable time thinking about clients who are *not* in crisis. I stress that there may be fleeting thoughts which intrude when they are away from work. The thoughts may be affectionate, or fearful and hostile. For example, a counselor may find herself looking forward to seeing a client she has seen for the last few weeks because during these sessions the counselor enjoyed listening to the client talk about her life and became interested in the characters in her client's life.

The first, and most difficult, step to be taken by the counselor is to notice and admit to herself that she seems to have the client on her mind for no apparent reason. Having made herself aware of her preoccupation with her client, the next step is to ask herself the question: "If there were ten other therapists involved in this client's care, would they look forward to their sessions with her in the way that I do?" It strikes me that this is a question which can be answered fairly objectively. If the answer is, "No," the counselor then moves on to the third step. She must ask herself, "Who does this client remind me of? Perhaps she has a particular mannerism, gesture, way of speech, or just something about her, that reminds me of a much loved figure from my past, or even someone who is presently in my life?" If the character from her personal life is identified, the counselor has to let herself know that she has been interacting with the client as if she were the identified character. With this knowledge, the counselor will be in a position to start to get to know the client afresh, and will have to face up to the fact that she has not yet begun to understand anything about the client, because she has been enjoying the sessions too much, from a there-and-then perspective rather than attending to the here-and-now. Unfortunately, these sessions had little to do with the client, so it is a matter of starting again.

It really is a problem the way people tend to relate to each other as though they are someone else. It may be that a friend introduces you to another friend and the person reminds you of someone you knew years ago and before you know it, you are responding to the person as if she were your old acquaintance. Very few of us know who anyone else is, since most of the time we are relating to people as though they are someone else. And in everyday life we get away with it. No one comes along and confronts us about this bizarre behavior.

No mental health officer suddenly appears while you are food shopping in the supermarket asking you to accompany him Downtown because you have been mis-identifying people close to you. That is what is so amazing about how much craziness society is able to tolerate. Society does not require us to keep each other in mind when we relate, just so long as we do not cheat each other or become violent. Those who begin therapy, though, to make sense of the madness going on around and within them, are treated with suspicion by their friends and relatives, the same people who related to the individual for so long as if he or she were somebody else. I think they are afraid *they* will be found out if one of them enters therapy. It is almost as if the person entering therapy is saying, "Okay, the game's up. For once and for all I am going to find out who I really am. Not who I am for *you*, my friends and relatives, but who I am for *me*." Having gone to all that trouble it would be tragic to find oneself in therapy with someone who related to their new client as though he or she were a much loved figure from the counselor's past. That really would be unfair.

The counselor who was preoccupied with her client may decide that if there were ten other therapists involved, all of them would probably be taken with this client since she is so easy to be with and very pleasant. Not only that, but she seems so appreciative of the counselor and makes her feel so adequate. Now that this conclusion has been reached, the counselor can resume the counseling sessions with this added knowledge and share it with the client in the following way:

THERAPIST: *(Listens to client)*

CLIENT: *(Talks about her week and then stops.)*

(Silence)

THERAPIST: *(Picks up on underlying feelings that have been expressed by client. Pause.)*

It's been four weeks since you've been coming for sessions and I've noticed that you find it easy to talk to me. It seems almost effortless for you to relate to me. I don't know if that's true of how you're experiencing the sessions.

CLIENT: *Oh, everyone finds me easy to talk to. People are always asking me to meet them for a drink, because they feel so comfortable with me. I don't have any problems getting along with people. That's not why I came here. No, my problem is that if I let people see the me **behind** the mask, they wouldn't want to spend any time with me at all.*

THERAPIST: *Right. So what you're saying is that you're not at all surprised to hear me say how easily you relate to me. That's not a difficulty for you. What's hard, though, is dropping the mask. It sounds like what you're saying is that what you need here is the chance to get in touch with those parts of yourself which you're not sure you like, and which you don't think other people will like either. You can do that here with me, because here in this relationship the important thing isn't about me liking or not liking you - the work we have to do here is for you to understand more about yourself, more about those parts of yourself you feel you and other people won't like so much.*

In that way the counselor's awareness of her preoccupation with the client prevented her from continuing a countertherapeutic relationship with the client which would in fact have been nothing other than a repetition of the past for the client without the benefit of new and meaningful understanding contributing to her self-exploration.

Obviously, the same principle can be used in reverse for clients that therapists dread to see. However, a further example will show how valuable the therapist's ability to be true to herself can be for clients. In this case the counselor had decided that if ten other therapists were involved, none of them would feel differently towards the client because he was an abusive and offensive man. The counselor believed that she was not alone in wishing to call in sick in anticipation of the sessions. She felt that her reactions were understandable. This awareness allowed her to behave differently in the next session. Having gone through the steps described in the previous example, she was able to be with the client in the next session in a non-defensive mode, not taking his verbal abuse personally.

THERAPIST: *(Listens to the client talking about his week)*

(Acknowledges his feelings)

It's been four weeks since you've been coming for sessions. I think it's true to say that the sessions have been difficult.

CLIENT: *Difficult! Difficult! Call yourself a psychologist do you? Of course, they've been difficult. All of you people are difficult. I suppose you're going to tell me you can't help. Just like everyone else. You people make me mad. You sit there looking so clever, but you're all the same. It's all right for you. What do you know?*

THERAPIST: *Yes, I can hear how exasperated you are. It seems like none of us are helpful and you doubt that I will be of any use to you because you expect me to say, " I can't help," just like other people have told you that in the past.*

CLIENT: *You know, you people make me laugh. None of you know what you're talking about. You come in here and tell me these sessions have been difficult. Of course they've been difficult. What do you expect?*

People have always told me I'm difficult. Even my own mother and father didn't want me. I got pushed around from home to home. I've been on my own my whole life. Never stayed anywhere for long. Nobody wanted to know. People like you don't want to know about people like me. I don't even know why I bother to come here.

THERAPIST: *As I've been listening to you today, I've better understood that of course our sessions would be difficult. You've explained that people have pushed you away throughout your life so that you've never had the opportunity to develop an easy relationship with anyone. You said that your mother and father rejected you and you got pushed around from home to home.*

But here in your therapy relationship with me, we can work together to better understand what your relationships have been like in the past, inasmuch as how they've not been satisfying for you, and perhaps that will make it possible for you to discover ways of establishing relationships in the future that may be more satisfying for you.

> *If you decide to continue with the sessions, that's the way I suggest we work together.*

CLIENT: *I don't think you can help and I don't think you really want to. Too many people have made me promises. I'm sure you can appreciate my scepticism. But I'll be here next week. You psychologists drive me crazy, but I'll give you another chance. Hey, what have I got to lose?*

In this example, it can be seen that the counselor's ability to take hold of her reluctance to be with the verbally abusive client allowed her to verbalize the difficulty to him. In turn, that allowed the client to describe in a more detailed way than previously what his life had been like. The counselor was in a non-defensive position and was listening carefully to what the client was describing, rather than being distracted by his insulting asides. By focusing on the important history of rejection, and not taking his insults personally, the opportunity arose for the therapist to feel some compassion towards her client. This feeling of compassion enabled her to stay in touch with his inner world and allowed for the contract to be made, whereby she made a psychotherapeutic commitment to work with him.

Summary of Day 1

Introductions enabled participants coming from various settings and locations to familiarize themselves with the people they would be working with on the course. The ground rules for the five days were established, and the course leader lectured on numerous aspects of nondirective psychotherapy, as described in the previous chapters of this book.

The differences between here-and-now and there-and-then material were identified, demonstrating how counselors risked relating to clients as though clients were characters from their personal lives. Special emphasis was placed on the concept of congruence so that participants quickly began to appreciate the difference between therapeutic and nontherapeutic (social) interactions. Detailed examples demonstrated how counselors could utilize their own fleeting thoughts, feelings and behaviors that were just beneath the surface to monitor whether or not they were being congruent within potentially psychotherapeutic relationships.

Day 2

The second day is almost always entirely devoted to skills practice. I begin with a demonstration of counseling a volunteer from the group, showing how I attempt to translate all that I have so far said into a psychotherapeutic nondirective facilitative interaction. Participants are in this way introduced to the format and purpose of the skills practice for the duration of the course.

Each brief session lasts ten or fifteen minutes, depending on the preference of the course participants. By focusing on the counselor's interventions, skills can be developed in giving the counselor feedback in terms of in what ways his or her interventions were helpful and in what ways they were not. From the outset, it is important for me to demonstrate that the task is to analyze the counselor's interventions to help participants be more specific as to what comprises a helpful psychotherapeutic intervention in terms of how it is communicated to the client.

Rogers' (1957) sixth condition of "The Necessary and Sufficient Conditions For Therapeutic Personality Change," is the driving force behind the skills practice - the communication to the client of the therapist's empathic understanding and unconditional positive regard is to a minimal degree achieved. And I put it this way. I indicate that it is not enough that two persons are in psychological contact and that one of them is congruent in the relationship and the other is incongruent; it is not enough that the counselor experiences unconditional positive regard for the client, nor is it enough that the counselor experiences an empathic understanding of the client's internal frame of reference; none of this is enough unless *the client* experiences the interaction in these ways.

How then can we know whether or not clients have experienced us in these ways? We cannot ask them because questions bring clients back to cognitive rather than emotional levels. That means we will be given intellectual accounts of how they *thought* they experienced us. I think of a question as a switch which serves as a gear shift from an emotional drive to a cognitive one. However, when counselors wait, they learn whether or not they were experienced as facilitative or prohibitive of clients' self-exploratory processes.

Clients do not experience counselors as having met the necessary and sufficient conditions for therapeutic personality change when sessions seem to be going round and round in circles in the following way: the client comes in and gives an account of something in his life. The counselor intervenes and the client repeats the story. After a number of interventions by the counselor it becomes apparent that although twenty minutes have passed, the counselor and client seem to be caught up in a struggle and the client's process has not been facilitated.

In these circumstances, I encourage participants to accept responsibility for not being facilitative, which means initially having to let themselves know that the session is stuck. Once the counselor can acknowledge that the session is stuck, he or she can then say to the client:

COUNSELOR: *You came in today and talked about a number of things and I have made various comments. However, I think it is right to say that my comments have not been helpful since we seem to be going round and round in circles.*

CLIENT: *Oh, that's all right, you're doing your best.*

COUNSELOR: *Yes, I would like to help. If you could bear to tell me once again, only this time I will listen without interrupting, because I recognize that you have something important to communicate.*

CLIENT: *(Repeats the story)*

The counselor keeps her word and does not interrupt. However, she notices the point at which she had intervened previously. As the client continues, the counselor appreciates that he is speaking about meaningful issues that are not directly related to the detail she found so intriguing that probably had more to do with her psychological process than the client's.

Allowing clients to work at their own pace

In this way, I am able to demonstrate to course participants the importance of *waiting* until clients have completed an idea before intervening. Many errors in counseling and psychotherapy sessions occur because counselors intervene while the client is still giving background information. In this way, many clients never get the opportunity to explore deeper material. Counselors who rapidly engage with clients on factual material stop the client's process so that counseling sessions risk becoming no more useful than social chats. Social chats frequently go round and round in circles, possibly because there is a sense of safety in not moving forward. It is not only the client's resistance that has to be overcome to make it possible for self-exploration, but often more significantly the unconscious resistance of the counselor.

In my courses, I devote much time to the issue of premature intervention, and use the following analogy. I ask the participants to imagine that they made arrangements weeks ago to meet an old friend for dinner at a Downtown restaurant. The day of the dinner date arrives, and it is the middle of winter, so that right after work instead of going home to relax and unwind, the two people have a commitment to meet. What follows are their plausible inner feelings and experiences within the first ten minutes of settling in at the restaurant:

JILL: *(Arrives on time. She feels cold and windswept having walked three blocks from her office. Her old friend Laura has not arrived yet).*

Jill thinks to herself . . . Good. I'm glad she's not here yet. At least I'll have some time to . . .

LAURA: *(Enters restaurant and sees Jill walking towards the Rest Room. She walks up to her). Hi, Jill. It's good to see you. Have you been here long?*

JILL: *Hi, how are you? No, no, I just arrived. Let's get seated. (**Her inner thoughts were: Oh dear! I really needed a bit of time to myself. I really don't want to be here. It's been such a hard day and I'd really prefer not to think about anything. I just want to go home and relax.**) I haven't seen you for such a long time. How's Jeff and the kids?*

LAURA: *Oh, they're fine. As a matter of fact I've got lots to tell you. So much has happened since we last met. I can't wait to fill you in. But first tell me about you. I've been hearing all good things about you. It sounds like your career has really taken off.*

JILL: *(Laughs) Who have you been talking to? (**Feels uncomfortable. Still unable to shake off feeling cold and beginning to get hungry now too. Asks herself . . . Why did we make this dinner date? I should have realized I'd be too tired and grumpy to socialize right after work.**) There isn't very much to say about that except that it's true that my career has really taken off and I'm feeling good about that. Come on Laura. Tell me your news. (Five minutes have passed)*

WAITRESS: *(Asks for and receives orders)*

LAURA: *(Tells her news enthusiastically)*

JILL: *(**Half listens to Laura and at the same time gradually settles in to restaurant. Has now recovered from the cold and wind, and looks forward to the meal. Lets herself get drawn into Laura's news and begins to enjoy her company, and no longer feels so bad about having made the**)*

arrangement in the first place.) *Laughs and makes friendly comments.*

LAURA: *Jill, I've been so looking forward to seeing you. Both of us are so busy. . . and time passes so quickly. (Pause) You seem a bit quiet and reserved tonight. Is there anything wrong?*

JILL: *You're right we do let too much time pass without getting in touch. The fact is I'm tired most nights after work. Things are developing very well at the moment, but I'm under a lot of pressure. Don't worry, I'm fine. It takes me a while to relax when I leave the office these days.*

WAITRESS: *(Food is served)*

LAURA: *And here I've been jabbering away.*

JILL: *That's been great. I feel much better now. And this food tastes so good. Once **I** begin to jabber there'll be no stopping **me**. So please tell me more. You know, I was wondering if you went to the reunion last week.*

LAURA: *Yes, and you were missed.*

JILL: *Oh, come on. Tell me everything. Who was there?*

(Ten minutes have passed, and Jill has now settled in and seems genuinely pleased to be there).

The above example speaks for itself. In counseling and therapy, very often in the first ten minutes of a fifty-minute or one hour session, clients are settling in, perhaps recovering from the cold weather outside, and stressful journeys. Indeed, also when obvious stressful circumstances in keeping appointments are absent, clients need time in the first part of the session to accommodate to the therapeutic setting.

I do not think it is either reasonable or helpful to intervene too soon, since it is not unusual for clients to begin sessions with material other than that which they wish to explore, simply as a way of getting started and getting used to being there again. My own view is that in every session, clients need time to check the therapist out again for trustworthiness in terms of getting a sense of whether or not the setting is really safe enough to explore some sensitive material. This process goes on unconsciously. Most clients do not literally sit there and ask themselves these questions. Instead, they respond to the setting. Therefore, those counselors and therapists who go for the initial material within the first few minutes may be precluding their clients from getting in touch with material that is just beneath the surface. The reason I take that so seriously is because what is now just beneath the surface may once again become repressed if clients are not facilitated in a way which enables them to get more in touch with themselves and less in touch with the therapist.

Directive therapists prefer to intervene right away, since they are prepared to take the consequences of losing less conscious material for the time being, believing that it will come up again. I am not usually prepared to take that risk in a deliberate way, and when I teach I warn participants of the dangers of not allowing clients enough time to get in touch with themselves before intervening.

When clients experience counselors as having met the necessary and sufficient conditions for therapeutic personality change, sessions have a different feel to them. Clients seem to be far more in touch with themselves rather than with their counselors. Facilitation has begun when clients seem scarcely aware of their counselors' presence.

For example, a client may have given an account of something in his or her life. The counselor waited until the client appeared to have completed an idea including fresh, new material before acknowledging the client's feelings in connection with the story, and then the client's self-exploration moved on with the awareness that the counselor was present and available. The atmosphere was such that the client was confident that the counselor was accepting him or her without judging and was genuine. The client sensed the counselor's wish to understand what the client was saying in terms of what it meant for the client in the context of his or her world, rather than what it meant to the counselor from the counselor's personal life experiences.

By way of demonstration, I also have in mind the wish to demonstrate the importance of giving clients enough space to discover something new about themselves for themselves. This is the goal I have in mind, which is realistically attainable, and at the same time which provides me with job satisfaction. That is why I teach participants to back off enough to make it possible within the working space for clients to safely self-explore. It may be something like:

CLIENT: *Today I see things differently.*

Although I've always known how inadequate I felt as a child in terms of not achieving at school, it is only now I recognize that same feeling of inadequacy when I am with my partner who is doing so well at work at the moment.

I've never really made that connection for myself before.

I emphasize that psychotherapy sessions are rarely dramatic. Usually they are solid hard work, well rewarded by counselors who exert enough self-discipline to allow clients to work at their own pace.

Summary of Day 2

All participants usually practised the counseling skills being taught bearing in mind the ground rules that were initially established. Participant observers practised giving each other feedback, thereby learning how to identify in what ways counselors' interventions were helpful and in what ways they were not.

The importance of Rogers' sixth condition for therapeutic personality change was kept in mind as participants learned how to be specific in saying how they reached their conclusions when providing feedback. Within that context, counselors learned the importance of *levelling* with their clients once the counselor was able to take hold of the fact that he or she was not being helpful. Being honest and up-front created opportunities for practising counselors to rectify their errors.

The importance of allowing clients to work at their own pace before too rapidly intervening was addressed throughout the section describing the second day and a detailed example illustrated the point. The temporary nature of feelings was emphasized so that practising counselors learned at the minimum to take a deep breath before intervening, recognizing that clients could be gearing up to communicate material that was hard to keep in conscious form. In that way participants experienced that given enough space the likelihood was increased that their clients could make their own self-discoveries within the psychotherapeutic relationship.

Day 3

By now all of the participants have been in the counselor's chair at least once for a ten or fifteen minute counseling session with a client. It is difficult learning these skills in front of a group and the participants quickly adapt to what appears to be more threatening than is so. It is hard for the participants to accept that the experience is only for the sake of learning and that people are not being evaluated. What each counselor provides for the course is the opportunity for participants to learn from the ways the interventions were helpful and not so helpful. Also, each counselor-client interaction provides the course leader with the opportunity to make numerous teaching points based on the huge range of issues that arise.

For example, participants in the counselor's chair report that they lose track of what the client is feeling and saying because the content reminds them of similar predicaments they are experiencing in their own lives. In that way, we are able to explore the difficulties in learning to be empathic, when people have been used to over-identifying with others in the listening process. This is a very powerful and at times painful way of learning how detrimental it can be to patients when health and mental health professionals over-identify with them rather than adopt an empathic understanding. Important discussions arise from these revelations.

At the beginning of the course I let the participants know that I am a psychoanalytic psychotherapist teaching person-centered courses and assertiveness workshops. I also let them know in advance that what I teach is in many ways more nondirective than person-centered therapy. I also state my differences with the person-centered approach in terms of the importance I attribute to maintaining clear boundaries in which the psychotherapeutic work can take place. That is why I make sure that they have all attempted the skills practice before watching a video-recording of Carl Rogers' work (*Video - "Three Approaches to Psychotherapy - Kathy"*, *Part 1, Carl Rogers, 1977*).

I ask them to study Rogers (1977), observing the ways his interventions are helpful and in what ways they are not. Their subsequent comments are fascinating. By this time they have become used to the idea of not asking questions, and they seem surprised at the questions he asked. They also notice the extent to which he vocalized, *"M-hm"*, and nodding is another feature that gets a fair amount of attention. I do, of course, point out how brave it is even for a psychotherapist as highly respected and well-known as Carl Rogers to work on video so that his work can be scrutinized, and we really do scrutinize it.

Issues participants raise arising from their various work settings

By now, some participants have begun to explore work issues and this is where the supportive aspect of the course becomes important. The adherence to the ground rules usually makes it possible for sensitive and painful issues to be explored to do with their work in this safe setting. There is some diversity in the types of issues that are explored, and the participants share in the responsibility for each one of them to benefit from the course. The cooperative spirit of the course has usually solidified by now. Numerous issues and concerns are raised. Most of them come up repeatedly on the courses I teach.

One of the most frequent concerns I hear, from physiotherapists, nurses, and occupational therapists, has to do with the dilemma of being person-centered with their patients when emotional issues arise, and absolutely directive when attending to the hands on part of the work. It is almost as though they feel too self-conscious and fear that their patients will think they are strange when they make the shift. I recommend that health professionals explain to their patients what is going on, in the following way:

PHYSIOTHERAPIST: *We have forty-five minutes today. I think it will be best if we spend approximately twenty-five minutes on the physiotherapy, and we can spend the rest of the time talking about the way you feel about all that's been going on for you since you were diagnosed.*

I stress the importance of **separating out the physical therapy from any work that is done on the patient's emotions**. The reason for this has to do with having heard from many therapists and nurses that patients talk very freely about their feelings when some other therapeutic procedure is taking place. I remind health professionals that it is not difficult to get people to talk. What does require skill is knowing how to respond to the patient's material. Therefore, I encourage them to risk getting less material from the patient, and putting off any discussion of the psychological aspects of the patient's condition until they have completed the other therapy or information-giving part of the session. In that way, the patient can make more choices about what he or she wants to discuss and can be certain that the material is being heard.

Many health and mental health professionals assume that as long as patients are talking about their feelings the catharsis will be beneficial. I disagree. In many ways, talking when unsure whether or not one is being heard, is often no better than talking to oneself where material goes round and round in unchanged form, keeping the person feeling wound up and misunderstood. It is no better than talking to one's beautician or hairdresser who has no counseling training. There are customers who, almost automatically, find themselves talking about their personal lives while some part of their body is being looked after, but rarely feel any different than they would have had they discussed the same personal issues with a friend. In other words, it is not a psychotherapeutic exchange. I discourage health and mental health professionals from trying to do two things at once, and in that way their patients will perhaps become more respectful toward their own psychological processes and take them more seriously.

Another frequent concern comes from **health and mental health professionals working in the community who see patients in their own homes**. Many participants have described situations where they allow themselves to get drawn in as if it were a social visit. I advocate maintaining the same boundaries on home visits as one would in a clinic. I arrive and leave on time. The client knows at the outset the length of the session and any socializing is discouraged simply by staying on track in terms of the reason for the visit. It is possible to manage the boundaries when seeing patients in their own homes who are unable to get out, due to long term illness or physical disability, and patients often appreciate it because it makes them feel less anxious about their role - *patients, or hosts or hostesses?* In the same way as it would be inappropriate for me to offer clients refreshments during their therapy sessions in my office, it is equally inappropriate to turn a home visit into a social occasion.

There are participants who work with the elderly who take a different view, and perhaps there are a few exceptions, but very few. If health and mental health professionals find themselves having too many exceptions to the rule, they do perhaps need to look more closely at the kinds of relationships they are developing with patients to examine to what extent they are professional.

At the beginning of this chapter, I stated that many participants express difficulties they have in leaving work at work. Many of them take home their sadness about patients who perhaps are not going to recover. Others take home the anxiety about lengthy waiting lists and feel guilty about the large number of patients awaiting treatment. I discourage them from taking on this guilt and anxiety. We talk about the way some professionals are made to feel responsible for their patients in their training. It is almost as though **the system deliberately instils guilt feelings into its health and mental health professionals to increase the likelihood that they will take on more patients than is realistic, and they do.** This of course frequently results in staff burnout. On the course, we try to look at these issues from a different perspective. The perspective has to do with health and mental health professionals taking better care of themselves. It is not for them to accept responsibility for another human being's misfortune which was not caused by them. I point out that there is something grandiose and unrealistic about these feelings and they do not help patients at all by taking feelings of guilt and anxiety home with them. It is stressed that it is really important to strike a balance between time spent on professional and personal issues so that they can take pleasure in outside relationships and interests and take care of their own needs. What is upsetting is that there seems to be very little support in the workplace. They carry a huge burden in the work they do often with little supervision.

Another question that comes up from time to time, particularly from physiotherapists has to do with **how to be with people who have made unsuccessful attempts on their lives,** and who then become patients on accident recovery wards as a result of their injuries which are often very serious. Sometimes they care for patients who are very angry with themselves for failing in their suicide attempts and subsequently become withdrawn. I recommend that health and mental health professionals quietly acknowledge how awful these patients feel, without pressing them for reasons for their self-destructive behavior. Usually, it is enough to be there in a nonjudgmental way accepting that the patient's life had been painful enough that action was taken that was intended to bring it to an end.

Once health and mental health professionals understand that getting information is not always the clever or helpful thing to do, they can begin to be with their patients with empathy, and gradually a feeling of calm is introduced within the patient-therapist relationship, rather than panic and desperation to make things all right that are not all right. In this way, participants often leave the course with a very different set of attitudes about what might be helpful and therapeutic from those they previously held.

I stress throughout the course that anyone can get information from another person. That does not require any particular skill. If one has decided to get as much information as they can from patients, they better know what they are going to do with it, and how this transfer of knowledge will ultimately be beneficial to patients. Participants have commented on the competitiveness that goes on among health and mental health professionals about who can get the most information from patients. The rivalry sets in fast where staff members who know more than the others behave as though they must be very competent to have found out so much. Sadly, they often have no idea what to do with this private information, except to religiously share it with the team, so as to share the ignorance, perhaps of what to do with it. As I have indicated repeatedly, getting information does not necessarily have very much to do with understanding its meanings in the context of people's lives, unless one is prepared to develop psychotherapeutic relationships with them.

Participants ask how they can be of help to their **clients whose verbal skills are limited for numerous reasons**. I urge them to attend to clients' feelings which can usually be recognized from their nonverbal communications, and once they have a sense of what emotions may be present to take the risk of naming them. For example, a health professional might very gently say to a client who is repeatedly banging a table and making angry sounds, "You seem very upset today. You're banging the table and you sound upset, and I can see that you seem troubled." Once feelings have been acknowledged, clients can perhaps move on. It may be that *upset* and *troubled* were the wrong words. In that case, the client may shake his head or change the sounds he has been making in which case the health professional could continue to acknowledge the client's feelings by saying, "Now you're banging the table harder and you sound as if I may have misunderstood you when I said you sounded upset and troubled. I may have got it wrong, but I am aware that you are feeling strongly about something right now, and if you want, I can stay with you for a little while, maybe the next ten minutes, in case you want to let me know some more about how you're feeling, or if you like, I'll just sit here quietly with you and you don't have to explain anything if you don't want to."

Mental health professionals frequently express **frustrations in working on psychiatric units with people with severe emotional disturbance where the emphasis is on medication and practical problems**. Rarely, in psychiatric units in the UK, are patients' symptoms explored in terms of their *deeper* meanings and significance. Instead, the attitude is that the symptoms must be got rid of as quickly as possible, by focusing on biological, social and practical precipitants. Less frequently is a joint attempt made by the team to facilitate patients' self-exploration with a view to understanding more about the emotional aspects of an individual's symptomatology and its meanings.

Psychiatric ward rounds that I attended rarely included sensitivity to patients' pain and fright. Considerable time was spent intellectualizing about the cluster of symptoms patients presented so that various labels were chosen to name the illness. The person often seemed to get forgotten when symptoms were discussed in isolation. Often, course participants are surprised when they hear me talking about hallucinations, and other distortions of reality in a way which reveals the likelihood that symptoms have meaning and represent feelings of intense pain and fear.

Acknowledging feelings is equally important for those who distort reality due to severe disturbance as it is for anyone else. Bringing a frightened and confused person into a room in front of eight or more team members so that the symptoms can be exhibited is neither a helpful nor humane intervention, let alone a respectful recognition of patients' pain. When team members acknowledge how frightened patients are, the reality of that recognition can be a first step to healing.

Some of the mental health professionals on my courses find it helpful to be reminded of some of Freud's (1949) basic concepts to do with the *id, ego,* and *superego.* By having in mind how much we have to deal with in terms of maintaining sufficient ego strength to hang on to reality, it perhaps reduces the distance between staff and patients. I am not surprised when I meet people who are out of touch with reality and in some psychotic state. What does surprise me is that so many people are able to maintain enough ego strength to stay with reality most of the time.

Just as I do not consider people who have heart attacks to be weird or feared, nor do I feel that way about people who have had *ego attacks.* I put mental health professionals in touch with their own *psychoses,* by reminding them how they reach that state during sleep while they dream. People experiencing florid psychotic states do not know whether or not they are dreaming. For some, they remain for long periods of time in that unreal and sometimes frightening frame of mind.

Participants recognize the importance of receiving more supervision and training, and they often leave the course feeling enthusiastic about furthering their psychotherapeutic skills so as to be more effective with their patients on psychiatric units.

I have endeavored to describe some of the issues participants raise, and how my responses to them are usually consistent with the ideas of treating patients respectfully with regard for their uniqueness as experiencing beings who, just like the rest of us, are doing the best they can.

Summary of Day 3

Numerous examples of boundary issues were raised by participants. The tendency to over-identify with clients' predicaments rather than taking an empathic stance; the dilemma of adopting a nondirective stance when the primary part of the work with clients was hands on, for example, nursing or physiotherapy; and maintaining professional boundaries on home visits.

Participants learned that a cathartic release could not necessarily be equated with a therapeutic experience. They discovered that while getting people to talk usually poses no problem at all, knowing how to work with the material therapeutically required a thorough background in psychological principles, as well as psychotherapeutic skill based on a thorough training.

Distressing situations were described by participants. These included treating patients' injuries as a result of unsuccessful suicide attempts; attending to the emotional needs of people with limited verbal skills, and to those who had, at least temporarily, lost touch with reality.

The need for health and mental health professionals to take better care of themselves, particularly to prevent burnout, was addressed. Much discussion took place of limited staff and team support, and the urgent need for ongoing supervision and training.

Day 4

The underlying messages of the course are about the *uniqueness of each individual,* the *dangers in making assumptions about people, being nondirective* and understanding people as *experiencing beings.* The mood is set to explore painful issues to do with racism and awareness of cultural differences. A distinction is made initially between prejudice and discrimination. It is emphasized that prejudice is an attitude, and discrimination is a way of behaving. Discrimination is practised by people who are prejudiced. The prejudice may or may not be within their awareness. While prejudices are deepseated and difficult to alter, discrimination is a behavior that can be controlled. It is possible for people to decide not to discriminate whether or not they are prejudiced.

Racism and discrimination

This part of the course seeks to extend participants' awareness of the devastating effects on people who suffer discrimination. Exploration of the subtle ways in which discrimination occurs is encouraged, so that each participant can make a conscious effort to resist colluding with discriminatory practices either in their care of patients, or their teamwork with colleagues. They are urged to get in touch with their own prejudices without getting sidetracked by guilt or shame. It is stressed that it is not possible to grow up in any society without *catching* the prejudices of the larger society. It is the denial of prejudice that is often most painful to those to whom it is directed. It is only when we are true to ourselves that we can behave in a nondiscriminatory way.

The tendency to overcompensate for cultural differences is usually addressed whereby health and mental health professionals visiting a family of a different cultural background than their own may make assumptions about the family and voice them. The person-centered approach is again advocated so that people are viewed as experiencing beings and make themselves known to us in their own ways, choosing whether or not cultural issues are at the time important or not, rather than being pushed to focus on a particular aspect of themselves for the counselor's sake rather than their own.

Having stressed the importance of individual differences, attention is drawn to the racial abuse experienced by health and mental health professionals from patients in their care. In London, it is not unusual for patients to call and complain if their nurse is black. Many community nurses, whose work includes bathing and toileting adult patients who are either acutely or chronically ill, are verbally abused in the process of administering care. Also, on hospital wards, nurses and other health and mental health professionals are vulnerable to overt racial abuse. It is important on the course to speak about racism openly. The here-and-now feelings of practising in a racist society need to be expressed. Otherwise painful feelings remain bottled up, and each working day becomes excessively stressful, increasing the likelihood of health problems as well as job dissatisfaction.

In my courses many participants hold posts which combine management and clinical responsibilities. By increasing their awareness of the racism which is experienced by staff and patients, perhaps a process of exploration with regard to how health and mental health professionals can be more supportive of each other will emerge and be facilitated. It seems to me that once racism is addressed at management levels, it will be more likely to filter through *via* patient care in terms of making staff more aware of their own attitudes and ways of communicating to groups of people to whom they may be prejudiced.

And people labeled 'schizophrenic', 'personality disorder', as well as 'paranoid', often find themselves to be victims of discrimination. There seems to be a reluctance on the part of the psychiatric community, as stated earlier, to respond to individuals so labeled as unique individuals who may benefit from a psychotherapeutic relationship. Instead textbook language of symptom clusters prevails, oftentimes limiting the kinds of services that will be offered.

Since the widespread availability of major tranquilizers designed to control behavior as well as reduce levels of distress, many health and mental health professionals put aside the necessity of understanding each patient in his or her own right. Instead, they latched on to the pill culture that was designed to target specific symptoms so that different pills were aimed at various groups of people. It was as if a voice was saying, "All the schizophrenics on the ward, line up on the left, all those with paranoid features, over there, and all those with personality disorders line up on the right. We can administer the appropriate drugs to each group without ever having to get to know any of them. Hooray for classification systems!"

By denying people their individual differences, the psychotropic drug culture dealt a further blow for people who were not getting on too well. I am not suggesting that we throw away the pills, but of course they can be used in conjunction with psychotherapeutic work, as early on as possible, to reduce the likelihood of people being ill in the long-term. Discrimination should not be tolerated; it is a behavior that gets acted out arising from the prejudices of a culture against groups of people who are victimized.

Day 5

By the last day participants have been briefly exposed to cognitive-behavior therapy and psychoanalytic psychotherapy, so as to at least have some idea of what the main contrasting approaches look like. These sections of the course provoke discussion about various aspects of their work from different perspectives. Responding to emotional content and processes which are just beneath the surface is, perhaps, the hardest part of the course, and the part which participants struggle with the most. By now participants have often developed some closeness and the sadness of the course ending prevails. There is also a sense of urgency to consolidate what has been learned before they get back into their work routine where much of what has been talked about and practised might be forgotten.

Participants leave feeling more confident about their counseling skills

Looking back over the five days participants are sometimes surprised by their changes in attitude and often pleased with their newly acquired counseling skills. Many leave with the idea that the skills may come in useful in part of their work, but certainly not in all of it. I teach it somewhat dogmatically so as to increase the likelihood it is understood. Then participants can take it away and use it with some flexibility as it pertains to their respective work settings.

Less experienced participants without any formal counseling training, as well as experienced therapists of differing orientations, feel deskilled at the beginning of the course which creates considerable tension and discomfort. Unfortunately, this is a necessary prerequisite to enable them to acquire new skills that are not simply modified versions of those they have already been using. There is undoubtedly a good deal of unconscious resentment towards me in the early stages of the course, but it seems to be used constructively, probably because of an underlying mutual trust that the skills will ultimately benefit both the participants and their patients.

And course endings are sad for me, too. So many people come and go, many of whom write and let me know if the skills are proving helpful in their work. My efforts are usually rewarded simply with the knowledge that for every ten people who complete my course, it is probably fair to say that half of them pass on the benefits to the numerous patients they see which means that what I teach creates a ripple in the ocean. What also motivates me is the recognition that participants leave knowing more about themselves. Teaching skills is one thing, but enabling people to discover more about themselves is very special. It is that aspect of the way I work with participants which for me is of particular significance.

To Conclude

Each five-day counseling skills course I have taught has been different. Just as it is impossible to accurately delineate developmental stages, I have been unable to accurately separate each day of the course, since there are recurring themes throughout, and depending on participants' specific work areas, the emphasis and order of issues will vary. However, I have described the content which most frequently is covered.

I have been fortunate to have Cheryl Gordon, a freelance writer, collaborate with me in writing this book. Therefore, she has participated in one of my assertiveness workshops and a five day course to contribute to her understanding of the relevant issues. The final chapter is a personal account of what it was like for her on the course, followed by her poem. I cannot say whether the course she attended was typical, just as I cannot generalize about the clients I see. What is important about her account is that the experiences belong to and are personal to her.

CHAPTER
ELEVEN

Being on the Course
by Cheryl Gordon (1993)

The beauty of being a freelance writer is that I have the freedom to explore, research and write about anything which I find fascinating and interesting, and assisting in the writing of this book has been no exception. Yet here there has been an added beauty, for while I have gained an insight into the subject of counseling skills training, the actual experience of participating in one of the five day courses, has allowed me to explore my own thoughts and feelings, which I have only ever acknowledged during my own personal therapy sessions.

Most of my writing, over the past few years, has enabled me to inform readers about things they may not already know. I have been able to do this through my work as a freelance writer for a national newspaper, and also through my work in the public relations industry writing promotional and news material for newspapers, trade journals and consumer magazines. I most recently wrote a feature for a *Time Out* publication about stereotyping which related to peoples attitudes and pre-conceptions of a person based on outward appearances, and in fact this tied in very well with the issue of prejudice and discrimination which we covered on the course. Before I had my children, now aged six and eight, I spent a few months working in a citizens advice bureau to fulfil my instinctive need to help people and keep them informed, but I didn't complete the initial training course because I became pregnant, and have since concentrated on my writing career.

So when I was invited by Sandra Delroy to collaborate with her in writing this book, I was excited about being given the opportunity to explore a subject which was of particular interest to me and, more so, to participate in one of her counseling skills courses. I was a little concerned that the group might feel uncomfortable about me being there, because I was not a health professional and I was worried about feeling alienated. My group was made up of physiotherapists, occupational therapists, unqualified counselors, a nurse, a psychologist and a welfare worker all from different backgrounds and nationalities, with different levels of expertise, and I really did feel like an intruder. But we established confidentiality at the outset, to dispel any fears that they may have had about me writing about them or anything that they said. We assured the group that although I was collaborating in writing a book about the way the course leader works and what she teaches, whatever they said within the group would remain confidential. They were assured that we would not reveal anything about them in the book and that if ever they felt uncomfortable and unable to speak about something simply because I was there, then they should let the group know immediately. Thankfully they seemed to be happy with that, and accepted me as an equal participant.

However, I was also carrying the worry of having to tell them that I knew the course leader personally since we were actually related. I wondered if they may have some uncomfortable feelings in thinking that maybe I was more a part of her than a part of the whole group, and this put me under quite a lot of pressure, even though I believed that it would be far easier for them to cope with me being her niece than to cope with me being a complete outsider, at most an intruder. But I wasn't sure. Incredibly, and what I find so difficult to explain, and even understand, is that all my anxieties were allayed, because not only were we all able to accept one another for whoever we were and whatever work we were doing, but we went over and above straightforward acceptance. We built up an intense bond and camaraderie so much so that by the end of the course it was somehow difficult for us all to say goodbye to each other. There was a feeling of empathy and understanding between us all and we all seemed to care about one another in a way that emphasized for me the fact that most members of the group were in the 'caring' professions.

I don't know if there was something special and unique about my particular group, but we bonded extremely well and the experience of being part of a group was more enjoyable than I had ever imagined. Even during our breaks and lunches away from the course leader, as students we stayed together without pairing up or splitting off into small groups. I loved the warm and positive feeling between us and the welcome element of humor and light-heartedness that ran throughout the group, which balanced well with the heavier, deeper and more intense levels of the course. I don't recall anyone complaining about the course at all and I don't know whether our enjoyment came from the personalities within the group itself, or whether it came from the way that the course was being taught. Maybe it was a combination of both, but I experienced a lovely sense of belonging, both at a participating student level during the course itself, and also at a social level when we took our breaks.

I am certain that all the group members will have their own memories about how we developed such a strong bond, but there was one incident in particular that I felt brought us all together. The course leader had made it quite clear to all participants, exactly what the course boundaries were in terms of starting and ending on time, and lunch and coffee breaks running to a particular time, and on the first day a couple of participants arrived late and saw that we had already started. So during our first break, which was actually our first opportunity to chat socially to one another, the conversation was able to flow freely because we were not pressurised into having to talk about who we were and what we did, but were able to form an instant link as we laughed and worried about which train and bus routes would get us there on time every day. These amusing debates of arriving on time continued throughout the five days, and although I felt that this must have been an important part of our bonding process, I didn't actually know the reasons why. All I knew was that the lateness of a couple of participants reflected upon us for the duration of the course and for me, this formed the basis of our strong group bonding.

As the days progressed and we talked more about the question of boundaries and setting limits I felt that it was becoming a particularly important issue for me, not only in relation to our group bonding, but also because of its relevancy to some of my own experiences of my relationships with others. I am someone with a 'listening ear' and I sometimes find that my personal space and time is invaded by 'phone calls from distressed friends looking for sympathy. While I am always happy to listen to them there are times when we go over and over the same issue week in and week out and I realise that, in fact, I am not helping them at all. Until now I have never known how to cope with this situation, but what I gained from the course was the knowledge that one really can't be a friend and a counselor at the same time. I have learned to tell my friends that they should seek professional counseling for their problems and not to hide them behind our friendship. As someone who is not a professional counselor I know that I can take the burden off their shoulders but I also know that I cannot really help them to understand their behavior. It would be far easier for me to say, "Okay you have fifty minutes, start talking, and then we must stop", because by setting these limits they would realize that they cannot telephone me whenever they like and expect me to listen to them for hours. So, instead of feeling guilty about sometimes wishing they would just leave me alone at 11.00pm, I now realize that I must make my boundaries clear and define my role as their friend and not their counselor.

But even as a sympathetic friend, there was something I learned about myself on the course that took me quite by surprise. I had always thought that I had a good 'listening' ear because so many of my friends have come to me with their problems. But what struck me most during the first listening skills exercise was that I had immense difficulty in actually listening to *exactly* what the client was saying and I began to think that maybe I wasn't such a good listener after all. It made me aware that while many of us can *hear* what people are saying, we may not actually be *listening*. To be able to listen to every word, every fact and every feeling, without getting side-tracked on the way, is an incredible skill. It was easy to listen for a while but then I became so interested in what was being said that I totally lost concentration as to how the other person was feeling, how they were expressing themselves, and what their body language was saying. I found myself listening for a while and then stopping to think, "Oh yes, I understand that, that happened to me," and before I knew it I had missed the next few things they had said. I was horrified to think that maybe I only pick up the interesting and important things for myself, which may not necessarily be the important things for my friends.

Since the listening experience left me feeling so uncomfortable with myself, when it came to volunteering to practise the skills as the 'counselor', I opted for nonparticipation. Also I didn't think I would be able to cope with making mistakes since I have a personal need to get things right first time and in view of the added pressure of my relationship with the course leader I knew I would feel self-conscious and embarrassed. While the other participants were already working in areas of counseling and had an immediate need to practise their skills, I felt that it was not vital and necessary for me at that time, but, because we were working as a fully integrated group I had some feelings of disloyalty and I felt I was letting the others down. Although it wasn't compulsory to participate in everything I confronted them with my feelings of guilt, and they reassured me that my observations and comments were extremely constructive, which made me feel more relaxed.

Even though I did not participate as a 'counselor' I found it fascinating to see the changes in people between the first day's skills practice sessions and the last, and how far people had moved towards the client-centered approach from where they had started. It was difficult for some of the group to remain neutral and nonjudgmental in order for the client to stay with their own feelings, because they were used to praising their clients, and in fact there was one fascinating moment relating to this. A lively member of the group sat in the 'client' chair and with a big beam on her face started to tell the 'counselor' about how wonderful she was feeling and how deliriously happy she was and for a few instants the 'counselor' was totally thrown because she got caught up with the excitement! While the 'counselor' was smiling, the 'client' continued with the enthusiasm, and when we discussed this particular interaction afterwards it became clear that had the 'counselor' responded in a less bubbly, less involved and entertained way, but in a more neutral way, then she would have seen that the 'client' was grappling with more painful underlying feelings. Remaining consistent with the underlying theme of the course, that each of us is unique, we all expressed our feelings and emotions in different ways and I could see how important it is for the counselor to remain neutral, nonjudgmental and non-biased. This theme came up again during the lecture on cultural issues and racism awareness, and I was deeply struck by how this issue was entirely consistent with the underlying theme of the course.

Although I was thoroughly enjoying my time on the course I became more introspective as the days progressed and I realised that I was beginning to express some of my inner thoughts during the skills practice sessions when I was being 'the client'. I really surprised myself because of my initial anxieties about how I would manage to bring up personal issues in view of my relationship with the course leader. As one of the participants said, "It is more difficult thinking of what you do NOT want to say as the 'client', rather than thinking of what you DO want to say, for fear of getting too deeply involved in something very personal". But the course leader made it quite clear that we didn't have to talk about anything personal at all, but interestingly enough we all did, and I don't know how much this release of personal issues had to do with the confidentiality built into the five days, or whether it was something to do with the warmth, empathy, trust and security that I felt running through my particular group. One member of the group said that she thought she would be scared to participate as a 'client' because she had so many apprehensions about having therapy for herself and coming from a family who didn't believe in making a fuss and covered everything up, she thought it too self-indulgent to self-explore. However, once she had been given the chance to self-explore a little during the five days, she admitted her sense of relief at being able to talk confidentially within the group and to find herself speaking quite openly about some personal issues. Deep down I felt quite pleased, because it seemed as though she experienced the same sense of security and trust within the group as I did.

This trust and sensitivity within the group became the focal point of the course for me and I was overwhelmed that even though the question of confidentiality between us had been discussed, the personal issues we brought up in the 'clients' chair were not transferred to the lunchtime 'pub' chair. We spent an hour together each day chatting about work, children, and where we lived, but we never ever discussed anything personal that had already been said in the 'chair', however tempting it was to say, "Tell me about such and such", or "It sounds as though you've been having a rough time". I think it would be impossible for anyone to imagine the experience of being with a group of people and just not talking about certain information because it had already been said when they were in the 'clients' chair, and I experienced this as deep trust, sensitivity, and respect.

When I brought up some of my own personal thoughts and feelings in the 'client' chair for the first time, I experienced an incredible sense of warmth and relief. It was tremendously comforting and reassuring to hear the counselor reflecting back my feelings and I felt as though there was somebody really trying to understand exactly what I was going through. The client-centered approach lends itself beautifully to the feeling that someone is being there with you and when I spoke of some difficult issues for me at that time, I was not fobbed off with, "There, there, you'll be okay," but felt that there was somebody listening without being critical, judgmental or patronizing. I thought, "It's okay for me to express my feelings and thoughts with this person. She understands me and I feel safe".

However, I did also experience the sense of feeling let down because while it was warming and comforting when the 'counselor' reflected my feelings back well, I was very aware that when my feelings were not reflected back correctly, and the 'counselor' got sidetracked by interesting facts, I was left in some discomfort instead of relief. I found that sometimes the facts that were picked up were not actually the points that were troubling me, and I had to begin my next sentence by trying to steer myself back onto the track that I really wanted to stay with. Then if the main issues were again not correctly reflected back, I was left talking about something which I really didn't want to talk about and then had no more to say. This left me thinking that it feels much better when the health professional is experienced in counseling skills, because when used correctly, the client-centered approach really did make me feel comfortable.

Spending so much time as a participant among a group of health professionals gave me quite an insight into the work that they do, and I was certainly left with a great deal of admiration for them. But what really upset me was that they all said that they had been given very little counseling skills practice in their training and that while counseling was becoming a more important part of their work, they weren't getting enough time and support within the workplace for being in a client/counselor relationship with their patients, primarily because they were restricted by budgets and time. I felt disillusioned to see that these extremely caring and genuine people weren't properly equipped to perform their helping roles in society, and I would like to think that if ever I should need to see a health professional they will be qualified to deal with my emotional issues.

I think that, because I had such admiration for the work that these health professionals were doing, it would be almost impossible for me to have gone through an experience such as this without searching within myself as to whether or not I would want to be a counselor. I started to analyse the way I am with people and whether I would want to spend my time helping people on an emotional level or whether I am content with helping them on a social and also practical level, such as informing through writing. I believe that the five days I spent with my group were some of the most valuable days of my life. I gained a wealth of information about myself, for which I will always be extremely grateful.

Saying goodbye to the members of the group on the last day was extremely difficult for me. I felt as though I had known everyone for years, not days. We had grown so close and experienced so much together, that I didn't want to lose that feeling of warmth, security and belonging. We had travelled along together just enough to get a glimpse of each others worlds, and I felt that just as we were settling into a routine of meeting every day and discovering more about ourselves and about each other, we had to suddenly break away from it all. I was left with a feeling of sadness and loneliness for a day or two afterwards and I missed the feeling of belonging, and the feeling of being able to be myself without criticism or judgment. It is difficult to explain to someone who has not experienced this, but it felt like a real sense of loss. For five days I had been part of a complete unit and then I had to leave the cushion of security and get back to reality where I had other responsibilities. We were complete strangers who had got to know each other so intimately that it was really quite difficult to accept that we had to let go and maybe never see each other again.

The multitude of feelings and emotions that I experienced during the five days were quite overwhelming, and so unexpected. From the anxieties of joining the group, the enjoyment and belonging, right through to the feelings of separation and loss, I gained, as a writer, the most beautiful insight into counseling and the counseling skills training of health professionals. But more rewarding than that, I also gained a remarkable insight into myself, which I hope will benefit me in the relationship I have with myself, and my relationships with others.

JUST BENEATH THE SURFACE

by Cheryl Gordon

Past experience, future hopes,
self-exploration, personal growth,
Uniqueness of experiencing beings with
sad,
happy,
mixed
feelings.

Intimacy, relationships,
close enough,
yet still apart,
together therapeutically,
separate boundaries from the start.

How vulnerable the client,
how tentatively we tread,
assessing,
knowing nothing,
like a book to be read.

The need to facilitate,
assess,
maybe both,
allows understanding, then personal growth.

Being empathic,
discreet,
and accepting,
responding through
listening,
repeating,
reflecting.

Starting at the beginning,
first experience, through to last,
getting back to the present
from the all important past.

Just beneath the surface
we have dreams and future hopes
exploring our emotions
for self-development and growth.

GLOSSARY

Aggressive:
Hostile or destructive behavior, often arising from low self-esteem that usually results in putting other people down

Anxiety:
An emotion characterized by feeling at odds with oneself; overall uneasiness and apprehension that something untoward is about to happen. The feelings are often motivated by conflicting motives that may be outside one's awareness

Assertive:
Clear, honest and direct behavior that usually results in respecting rights of self and others and takes the mystery out of relating. Stating concisely what one means and wants; responsibly negotiating with others, striving towards acceptable compromise while taking each other's feelings into account

Behavior therapy:
A psychotherapeutic or counseling approach that seeks to eliminate symptoms or maladaptive *learned* responses through new types of learning

Catharsis:
An act of purging; getting rid of; bringing to consciousness, followed by its expression and subsequent elimination

Classical conditioning:
A learning process where a response becomes attached to a conditioned (previously neutral) stimulus

Cognition:
The process of knowing; within one's awareness

Conditions of worth: Acceptance of other is conditional on his or her conformity to particular behaviors, beliefs and attitudes

Congruence: Behaving, feeling and thinking in ways that are *consistent* with one's self-image; being true to oneself

Contracting: Entering into a relationship whereby on the one part, the counselor agrees to offer psychotherapeutic expertise and on the other part, the client agrees to work on his or her psychological issues. Joint responsibility is taken for defining goals as well as the commitment to work towards them

Directive: Psychotherapeutic approaches where the counselor directs the course of sessions with questions and comments that usually have more to do with the counselor's psychological processes than the client's

Empathy: Being with another and sensing his or her experience *as if* it were one's own, in order to better understand the way the other experiences his or her inner and outer worlds

External frame of reference: Trying to understand clients' communications according to the counselor's view of the world, based primarily on the counselor's personal and professional experiences of living

Facilitative: Makes easier

FHSA: Family Health Service Authorities administering primary health care services in the UK

Here-and-now: That part of the psychotherapeutic process which is primarily concerned with relationship issues between the counselor and the client; the ongoing process of relating includes but is not limited to working through issues of confidentiality, length and frequency of sessions, appointment times, fees, missed appointments, lateness, interruptions due to holidays, etc.

Humanistic psychology: Psychological approaches that focus on qualities that distinguish human beings from other animals. Those qualities include desires for self-worth, dignity, and becoming self-actualized or a fully functioning person

Hysteria: Uncontrollable fear or emotions; a condition that was usually identified in women. The concept has become invalid for many counselors because of the way it has been used to derogate women

Hysterical: Impressionistic and global style of responding to stimuli; a personality style that is associated with the defense mechanism of repression

Iatrogenic illness: Condition involving adverse effects that could have been avoided by proper and judicious therapeutic care; the term usually relates to medical interventions

Incongruence: Mismatch between one's self-image (e.g. "I am a fair person,") and one's experience, that is, thoughts, feelings, ideas and behaviors that at times contradict the less conscious views individuals have about themselves. The incongruence produces anxiety

Internal frame of reference: Trying to understand clients' communications according to the client's view of the world, based primarily on the client's experiences of living within the context of his or her inner and outer worlds

Interpersonal: Involving relations between persons

Intrapsychic: Within the mind

Just beneath the surface: Preconscious; the level of awareness of which one is scarcely aware; fleeting thoughts, feelings, memories and ideas that are accessible to consciousness, if required

NHS: National Health Service in the UK

Nondirective: A psychotherapeutic stance whereby counselors follow and attempt to stay with the client's psychological process, rather than directing the course of a session with specific questions

Nontransference: Clients perceptions and reactions to the therapist which are valid and arise from nonconflicted areas of functioning (Langs, 1978)

Operant conditioning: A learning process whereby existing behaviors are strengthened or weakened through various reward and/or punishment programs

Organismic valuing process: A concept used in person-centered therapy which describes an ongoing process which other schools of therapy would describe as unconscious, where a person constantly monitors his or her experience in an attempt to move towards becoming a fully functioning person

Paranoia: Usually characterized by exaggerated mistrust and suspicion of others which become delusional beliefs of persecution or grandeur; other areas of functioning may remain intact

Personality disorders: A style of relating that often causes social conflict, and is associated with various areas of disturbance that may be emotional, cognitive and motivational. The term is frequently used inappropriately as a catch-all phrase for clients who are difficult to treat by inadequately trained staff. Much of the disturbance seen in the client may arise from very lengthy delays or a total absence of appropriate psychotherapeutic intervention

Person-centered therapy: A humanistic psychotherapeutic approach that is facilitative, emphasizing personal growth work in a nondirective, non-judgmental and empathic relationship

Psychoanalytic psychotherapy: A psychotherapeutic approach that emphasizes unconscious processes so as to make what was unconscious conscious, enabling clients to become more integrated through the emotional and cognitive insights emerging from the transference and its ongoing interpretation

Psychodynamic psychotherapy: A psychotherapeutic approach that emphasizes unconscious processes so as to make what was unconscious conscious. Often, there may be less emphasis on transferential issues, but for some psychodynamic therapists their approach shares the definition given above for psychoanalytic psychotherapy

Psychopathology: The study of maladaptive behavior

Psychosis: Conditions which are caused by severe psychological disturbances. There is loss of contact with reality and an inability to function in the environment

Psychotropic: Antipsychotic and antidepressant drugs that seem to alter the chemical substrates of synaptic transmission or axonal conduction within the central nervous system

Symbiosis: The association and attachment of two different organisms to each other

Sympathy: Offering condolences and responding in terms of how the sympathizer feels about another's situation or loss, without necessarily getting in touch with the client's feelings and inner experience

Transference: A component of the client's relationship to the counselor whereby the client's perceptions of the counselor, as well as responses, are distorted based on unconscious fantasies, memories and defence mechanisms. These distortions may derive from past relationships. They are communicated in some derivative form (Langs, 1978)

True to onself: Becoming more open to one's experience; it is the polar opposite of defensiveness. "To be that self which one truly is," moving away from facades, oughts, pleasing others, and meeting others' expectations, but instead in the process of self-direction, acceptance of others, and trust of self (Rogers, 1961)

Unconditional positive regard: Accepting the other without judging. An attitude of caring and unselfish regard free from demands for anything in return (e.g. "I care about you because you are human.")

REFERENCES

Alexander, F., French T. *et al.*, "The principle of corrective emotional experience." In: **Psychoanalytic Therapy. Principles and Applications.** New York: Ronald Press, 1946 pp 66-70.

British Association for Counselling **The Counselling and Psychotherapy Resources Directory.** Rugby: BAC, 1996

The British Pyschological Society **The Register of Chartered Pyschologists (Incorporated by Royal Charter).** Leicester: The British Psychological Society, 1995

Beck, A.T. **Cognitive Therapy and the Emotional Disorders.** New York: International Universities Press, 1976

Berardo, Donna Hodgkins. "Bereavement and Mourning." In Wass, Hannelore, Berardo, Felix M. and Neimeyer, Robert A. (Eds.) **Dying *(Facing the Facts).*** Second Edition. Washington: Hemisphere Publishing Corporation, 1988

Butler, Pamela E. **Self-Assertion for Women** (Revised Edition) San Francisco: Harper, 1992

Delroy, Sandra. "Attitudes Toward Confidentiality Among Clinical Psychologists in London, England." (Unpublished clinical research project), 1984

Dicaprio, Nicholas S. **Personality Theories: guides to living.** Philadelphia: W.B. Saunders Company, 1974

Donnelly, Katherine Fair. **Recovering From the Loss of a Parent.** New York: Dodd, Mead and Company, 1987

Ellis, Albert. **Humanistic Psychotherapy: The Rational-Emotive Approach.** New York: McGraw-Hill Book Company, 1973

Foster, Suzanne and Smith, Pamela. **Brief Lives.** London: Arlington Books (Publishers) Ltd., 1987

Freud, S. "Recommendations for physicians on the psychoanalytic method of treatment." In F. Rieff (Ed.). **Therapy And Technique.** New York: Collier Books, 1963 (Originally published 1912)

Freud, S. "Further recommendations in the technique of psychoanalysis: observations on transference love." In F. Rieff (Ed.) **Therapy And Technique**. New York: Collier Books, 1963 (Originally published 1915)

Freud, S. **The Standard Edition of the Complete Psychological Works.** London: Hogarth Press, 1963

Freud, S. "The ego and the id." In **Standard Edition of the Complete Psychological Works of Sigmund Freud,** 19, London: Hogarth Press, 1963

Freud, S. **An Outline of Psychoanalysis.** New York: W.W. Norton, 1949

Freud, S. **Introductory Lectures on Psychoanalysis.** New York: W. W. Norton & Company, 1966

Fromm-Reichmann, F. **Principles of Intensive Psychotherapy.** Chicago: The University of Chicago Press, 1950

Goldfried, M.R. and Davison, G.C. **Clinical Behavior Therapy.** New York: Holt, Rinehart & Winston, 1976

Greenacre, P. "The role of transference." In P. Greenacre, **Emotional Growth.** Vol II New York: International Universities Press, Inc., 1971 (Originally published 1966)

Jewett, Claudia. **Helping Children Cope With Separation and Loss.** London: B.T. Batsford Ltd., 1984

Kvarnes, Robert G. and Parloff, Gloria H. (Eds.) **A Harry Stack Sullivan Case Seminar (Treatment of a Young Male Schizophrenic).** New York: W.W.Norton & Co., 1976

Langs, R.J. **TheTechnique of Psychoanalytic Psychotherapy**. Vol I. New York: Jason Aronson, Inc., 1973

Langs, R.J. **The Technique of Psychoanalytic Psychotherapy.** Vol.II. New York: Jason Aronson, Inc., 1974

Langs, R. "The therapeutic relationship and deviations in technique." In R. Langs (Ed). **Classics In Psychoanalytic Technique.** New York: Jason Aronson, Inc., 1981 (Originally published 1975)

Langs, R. **The Bipersonal Field.** New York: Jason Aronson, Inc., 1976

Langs, R. **The Listening Process.** New York: Jason Aronson, Inc., 1978

Langs, R. **Psychotherapy: A Basic Text.** New York: Jason Aronson, Inc., 1982

Lazarus, Arnold. **The Practice of Multimodal Therapy**. New York: McGraw Hill Book Company, 1981

Mahler, M., Pine, F., and Bergman, A. **The Psychological Birth of the Human Infant.** New York: Basic Books, 1975

Maslow, Abraham. **Motivation and Personality.** 2nd ed. New York: Harper & Row, 1970

Mearns, Dave and Thorne, Brian. **Person-Centred Counselling In Action.** London: Sage Publications, 1988

Meichenbaum, D.H. **Cognitive Behavior Modification**. New York: Plenum, 1977

Milner, M. "Aspects of symbolism in comprehension of the not-self." Abstracted in R. Langs. **The Therapeutic Interaction.** Vol.I. New York: Jason Aronson, 1976 (Originally published 1952)

Nelson-Jones, Richard. **The Theory and Practice of Counselling Psychology.** London: Holt, Rinehart and Winston, 1982

Nelson-Jones, Richard. **Practical Counselling Skills.** London: Holt, Rinehart and Winston, 1983

Palmer, Elsie and Watt, Jill. **Living and Working With Bereavement (*Guide for Widowed Men and Women*).** Calgary: Detselig Enterprises Ltd., 1987

Rogers, Carl R. **Client Centered Therapy.** Boston: Houghton Mifflin Co., 1951

Rogers, C.R. "The necessary and sufficient conditions of therapeutic personality change." **Journal of Consulting Psychology** 21, 1957

Rogers, Carl R. **On Becoming A Person.** Boston: Houghton Mifflin Co., 1961

Rogers, C.R. "A client-centered/person centered approach to therapy." In Kutash, L. and Wolf, A. (Eds) **Psychotherapists Casebook: Theory And Technique in Practice.** Jossey-Bass Inc., 1986

Schoenberg, B.M. (Ed.) **Bereavement Counseling (*A Multidisciplinary Handbook*).** Westport: Greenwood Press, 1980

Searles, H. "The effort to drive the other person crazy — an element in the aetiology and psychotherapy of schizophrenia." In H. Searles, **Collected Papers on Schizophrenia and Related Subjects.** New York: International Universities Press, 1965

Shapiro, David. **Neurotic Styles**. New York: Basic Books, 1965

Skinner, B.F. **Beyond Freedom and Dignity**. New York. Alfred A. Knopf, 1971

Stroebe, Wolfgang and Stroebe, Margaret S. **Bereavement and Health** (*The Psychological and Physical Consequences of Partner Loss)*. Cambridge: Cambridge University Press, 1987

Watson, John. **Behaviorism.** Revised Edition. New York: Norton, 1930

Will, Otto. "Human relatedness and the schizophrenic reaction." **Psychiatry**, 22, 1959

Wilson, G.T. & Evans, I.M. "The therapist-client relationship in behavior therapy." In Franks, E. & Wilson, G.T. (Eds.) **Annual Review of Behavior Therapy**, 1976

Winnicott, D.W. **The Maturational Process And The Facilitating Environment.** London: The Hogarth Press, 1965

Worden, William. **Grief Counseling And Grief Therapy.** New York: Springer Publishing Company, Inc., 1982

VIDEO

Rogers, Carl R. and Kathy Part I Psychotherapy: **Three Approaches To Psychotherapy: Three Approaches II.** Produced by KOCE TV Channel 50 Coast Community College District, Shostrum Psychological Films, 1977